Christopher Long | THE NEW INTERIOR

Christopher Long

The New Interior

Viennese Domestic Design and the Beginnings of the Wiener Wohnkultur, *1907–1914*

KANT

For Claudia

Contents

List of Illustrations

Fig. 1. Ludwig Hevesi, 1905. Photo by Josef Löwy. Wien Museum, Inv. Nr. 132162.

Fig. 2. Adolf Loos, caricature by Carl Leopold Hollitzer, with an inscription from Peter Altenberg, 1908. Wien Museum, Inv. Nr. 94921.

Fig. 3. Adolf Loos, *Wohnungswanderungen*, Vienna, 1907. Brochure. Wienbibliothek im Rathaus, Vienna, Inv. Nr. 224.719.

Fig. 4. Adolf Loos, *Wohnungswanderungen*, "Zweiter Tag," n.p. Wienbibliothek im Rathaus, Vienna, Inv. Nr. 224.719.

Fig. 5. Adolf Loos, apartment of Rudolf Kraus, Vienna 1., Nibelungengasse 13, 1907. Photo: Martin Gerlach, jun. Adolf Loos Archiv, Albertina Museum, Vienna (hereafter ALA), 3120.

Fig. 6. Adolf Loos, apartment of Dr. Hermann and Dr. Eugenie Schwarzwald, Vienna 8., Josefstädter Straße 68, 1905, altered in 1909. Photo 1930, by Martin Gerlach, jun. ALA, 3137.

Fig. 7. Adolf Loos, "Wohnungs-Moden," *Frankfurter Zeitung,* Zweites Morgenblatt, 8 December 1907, 1.

Fig. 8. Josef Hoffmann, 1903. Photo by Friedrich V. Spitzer. Museum für angewandte Kunst, Vienna (hereafter MAK), WWF 137-1-2.

Fig. 9. Wiener Werkstätte showroom, Vienna 7., Neustiftgasse 32–34 ca. 1904–5. MAK, WWF 137-21-1.

Fig. 10. Wiener Werkstätte showroom, Vienna 7., Neustiftgasse 32–34, ca. 1905. MAK, WWF 105-279-2.

Fig. 11. Josef Hoffmann, reception hall, seen from the garden side, Kunstschau 1908, Vienna. From *Moderne Bauformen 7*, no. 7 (1908): 364.

Fig. 12. Josef Hoffmann, smoking room (Room 44), Kunstschau 1908, Vienna. From *Moderne Bauformen 7*, no. 7 (1908): 371.

Fig. 13. Josef Hoffmann, children's bedroom in white, Kunstschau 1908, Vienna. From Moderne Bauformen 7, no. 7 (1908): 373.

Fig. 14. Josef Hoffmann, Austrian Pavilion at the 1914 Werkbund exhibition, Cologne. From Moderne Bauformen 13 (1914): 387.

Fig. 15. Adolf Loos, "Lotusornament," student drawing from the State Trade School (K. k. Staatsgewerbeschule Reichenberg, Abteilung Baumeister), Reichenberg, dated November 5, 1886. ALA, 838.

Fig. 16. Josef Hoffmann, plaster relief (detail), exhibited at the Fourteenth Secession Exhibition, 1902. Österreichische Nationalbibliothek, Vienna, 213.369–B.

Fig. 17. Richard Schaukal, 1924. Photo by Hermann Clemens Kosel. Österreichische Nationalbibliothek, Vienna, NB 530692-B.

Fig. 18. Oskar Strnad, self-portrait, ca. 1905. Oil on board, 45.5 × 29.5 cm. Wien Museum, Inv. Nr. 103884. Photo: Birgit and Peter Kainz.

Fig. 19. Oskar Strnad, cover for *Wiener Türmer* magazine, 1904. Collection Christopher Long.

Fig. 20. Oskar Strnad, competition design for a synagoge in Triest, 1904. Motto: "Spiagge Adriatiche." Pen and ink and watercolor on paper, 36.7 × 53.8 cm. MAK, K.I. 13891.

Fig. 21. Oskar Strnad and Oskar Wlach, Hörandner apartment building, Vienna 7., Stuckgasse 14, 1910–11. Photo: Wolfgang Thaler.
Fig. 22. Oskar Strnad, living room in Strnad's own apartment on the Ungargasse, Vienna 3., 1909. MAK, K.I. 13831-1.
Fig. 23. Oskar Strnad, drop-front secretary, cabinet on stand, and chair in Strnad's apartment on the Ungargasse, Vienna 3., 1909. MAK, K.I. 13832-18.
Fig. 24. Oskar Strnad, ladderback armchair, designed ca. 1909; this example ca. 1912. Beechwood with braided straw seat, 105 × 63.5 × 47 cm. MAK, H2622.
Fig. 25. Ernest Gimson, ladderback armchair, made ca. 1892–1904. © Victoria & Albert Museum, London, CIRC.232-1960.
Fig. 26. Oskar Strnad, *Der Parthenon*, 1907. Lithographic print, K.k. Hof- und Staatsdruckerei, Vienna. Collection Christopher Long.
Fig. 27. Josef Hoffmann, Austrian Pavilion at the International Art Exhibition, Rome, 1911. Österreichische Nationalbibliothek, Vienna, Pk1450b, 2.
Fig. 28. Oskar Strnad and Viktor Lurje, garden room (Interior I) at the Second Exhibition of Austrian Applied Art at the Austrian Museum for Art and Industry, Vienna, 1910–11. Photo: Bruno Reiffenstein. MAK, K.I. 7781-27.
Fig. 29. Oskar Strnad, Josef Frank, Hugo Gorge, and Viktor Lurje, Room 2 at the Winter Exhibition at the Austrian Museum for Art and Industry, Vienna, 1911–12. Photo: Bruno Reiffenstein. MAK, K.I. 7826-22.
Fig. 30. Josef Frank, Hugo Gorge, Viktor Lurje, Oskar Strnad, and Oskar Wlach, Room 2 at the Winter Exhibition at the Austrian Museum for Art and Industry, Vienna, 1911–12. Photo: Bruno Reiffenstein. MAK, K.I. 7826-21.
Fig. 31. Catalogue page listing Strnad and Lurje's contribution to the Winter Exhibition at the Austrian Museum for Art and Industry, Vienna, 1911–12. *Ausstellung Österreichischer Kunstgewerbe 1911–1912*, exh. cat. (Vienna: K.k. Österreichisches Museum für Kunst und Industrie, 1911), 7.
Fig. 32. Oskar Strnad, grave marker for the Thenen family, 1909. MAK, K.I. 13841-9.
Fig. 33. Oskar Strnad, grave marker for Samuel Jakob and Martha Strnad, 1908. MAK, K.I. 13841-1
Fig. 34. Oskar Strnad, garden room (Room XVI) at the 1912 Spring Exhibition at the Austrian Museum for Art and Industry, Vienna. Furniture executed by Carl Bamberger; brickwork, floors, and walls by Brüder Schwadron. MAK, K.I. 7835-27.
Fig. 35. Oskar Strnad, garden room (Room XVI) at the 1912 Spring Exhibition at the Austrian Museum for Art and Industry, Vienna. Photo: Bruno Reiffenstein. MAK, K.I. 13823-4.
Fig. 36. Oskar Strnad, garden room (Room XVI) at the 1912 Spring Exhibition at the Austrian Museum for Art and Industry, Vienna. Photo: Bruno Reiffenstein. MAK, K.I. 13823-5.
Fig. 37. Wilhelm Friedrich, wall painting framing the entrance to Room XX at the 1912 Spring Exhibition at the Austrian Museum for Art and Industry, featuring the displays of the Vienna School of Arts and Crafts. *Deutsche Kunst und Dekoration* 31 (October 1912–March 1913): 179.

Fig. 38. Robert Örley, garden room (Room XV) at the 1912 Spring Exhibition at the Austrian Museum for Art and Industry. Chairs and tables executed by Pressstoff-Möbel-Gesellschaft M.B.H., Vienna. MAK, K.I. 7835-22.
Fig. 39. Josef Hoffmann, dining room (Room IX) at the 1912 Spring Exhibition at the Austrian Museum for Art and Industry, executed by J. Soulek, Vienna. *Deutsche Kunst und Dekoration* 31 (October 1912–March 1913): 183.
Fig. 40. Josef Frank, living room (Room XIII) at the 1912 Spring Exhibition at the Austrian Museum for Art and Industry. *Deutsche Kunst und Dekoration* 31 (October 1912–March 1913): 191.
Fig. 41. Oskar Strnad, salon, Fritz Hirsch Apartment, Vienna 1., Reichsratsstraße 1, 1913. MAK, K.I. 13829-6.
Fig. 42. Oskar Strnad, commode, Hirsch Apartment. MAK, K.I. 13829-9.
Fig. 43. Oskar Strnad, dining room, Hirsch Apartment. MAK, K.I. 13829-11.
Fig. 44. Oskar Strnad, sideboard, Hirsch Apartment. MAK, K.I. 13829-18.
Fig. 45. Oskar Strnad, children's room, Hirsch Apartment. MAK, K.I. 13829-26.
Fig. 46. Oskar Strnad, living room in the Wilhelm Hellmann Apartment, Vienna 1., Rathausstraße 17, Vienna, 1914. MAK, K.I. 13826-16.
Fig. 47. Oskar Strnad, bedroom, Hellmann Apartment. MAK, K.I. 13826-1.
Fig. 48. Oskar Strnad, secretary, Hellmann Apartment. MAK, K.I. 13826-4.
Fig. 49. Oskar Strnad, armchair, Hellmann Apartment. MAK, K.I. 13826-7.
Fig. 50. Josef Frank, living room (Room XIII) at the 1912 Spring Exhibition at the Austrian Museum of Art and Industry, Vienna. Photo: Bruno Reiffenstein. MAK, K.I. 7835-31.
Fig. 51. Oskar Strnad, living room in an apartment in Vienna 19., 1912. MAK, K.I. 13825-1.
Fig. 52. Oskar Strnad, office in an apartment in Vienna 19., 1912. MAK, K.I. 13825-2.
Fig. 53. Oskar Strnad with Oskar Wlach, ground-floor plan of the Wassermann House, Vienna 19., Paul-Ehrlich-Gasse 4, 1912–15. MAK, K.I. 13915-1.
Fig. 54. Oskar Strnad with Oskar Wlach, living room, view toward the music space, Wassermann House, 1912–15. MAK, K.I. 138.34-5.
Fig. 55. Oskar Strnad with Oskar Wlach, living room, Wassermann House. *Innen-Dekoration* 29 (January–February 1918): 20.
Fig. 56. Oskar Strnad, elevation of the wall in the Wassermann House, 1914. MAK, K.I. 13862-1.
Fig. 57. Oskar Strnad (Strnad, Wlach, Frank), office, ca. 1914. MAK, K.I. 14306-10.
Fig. 58. Josef Frank in his reserve officer uniform, 1913. Identification card for the Austria State Railways. Albertina, Josef Frank Archiv 186. Courtesy of Susanne Eisenkolb.
Fig. 59. Josef Frank, music and dining rooms, Josef and Anna Frank Apartment, Vienna 4., Wiedner Hauptstraße 64, 1913. MAK, K.I. 14306-15.
Fig. 60. Josef Frank, living room, Josef and Anna Frank Apartment, 1913. MAK, K.I. 14306-9.
Fig. 61. Hugo Gorge, hall, before 1921. MAK, K.I. 8309-13.
Fig. 62. Otto Wagner, proposed guest room for the Hotel Wien on Karlsplatz, 1913. Wien Museum, I.N. 139711.

Preface

For not quite seven years, just prior to World War I, a small group of designers in Vienna explored the possibilities of a new form of interior, a new way of living in the modern world. The three towering figures of this brief but extraordinary moment were neither friends nor collaborators, and two of them were avowed enemies. Josef Hoffmann and Adolf Loos, despite their closely shared backgrounds, had very different, and often competing, visions about what it meant to make a modern interior. For nearly a decade before, and long after the time recounted in this book, the two men squabbled, periodically hurling abuse at each other. The third, and by far the least well known—Oskar Strnad—avoided these quarrels, but it was he who offered perhaps the most radical restatement of modernity and living.

Concealed not far below the surface of these three figures' words and works were most of the strands of what would come after in design: the quest for a new purity, the possibilities of forging an attachment to the past, and the effort to reinsert "livability"—which is to say, comfort, both physical and psychological—into the domestic setting, while still embracing the concept of a modern lifestyle.

In the immediate run, Hoffmann's early pursuit of a new reductivness triumphed: the *Neue Sachlichkeit* and the Bauhaus of the 1920s and beyond would, for many, define what it was to be authentically modern. But Loos, and even more, Strnad, posited a design aesthetic that somehow made recourse to the past while thinking very hard about how we should live; their efforts would coalesce in a new design direction, the *Wiener Wohnkultur* (Viennese living culture). It would shape the look of many Viennese interiors in the 1920s and 1930s, and it would come back with remarkable power in the late 1930s. It was first expressed in the movement we know as Scandinavian Modern and later, more directly, in the Postmodern. Today, both directions are part of the faith of many interior designers, though not always articulated with the same clarity.

More meaningful for our time, though, is another idea that was spawned in the Vienna of those years: that the most important feature of modern life is not uniformity but multifariousness. For those searching for the seeds of today's multiculturalism, the beliefs of Loos and Strnad (and even Hoffmann) are not a bad place to look. They were not the only progenitors of today's cultural diversity by any means, but they remain, if one cares to look closely enough, some of its early makers.

The story I tell here moves quickly, even with broken speed. In a short time, in a place that was surprisingly small and intimate, and with a limited cast of characters, the discussion about what should constitute the modern interior took place with stunning force. The details sometimes conceal the true import of what was taking place. I seek to show just how exceptional and predictive it all was.

Austin 2024

Chapter 1

The False Secession

In late November 1907, Ludwig Hevesi published an extensive profile of Adolf Loos in the Viennese daily newspaper *Fremden-Blatt*. Hevesi was the associate editor of the paper's arts section (fig. 1). He was then one of the city's most authoritative–and feared–art critics. His words could build or destroy careers, facilitate new movements or thwart them altogether.[1] His insightful reviews had propelled the success of the Vienna Secession. From the first moment when Gustav Klimt, Joseph Maria Olbrich, Josef Hoffmann, and their fellow *revoltés* inaugurated their movement, he had lent them the considerable weight of his support, explicating their ideas and praising their efforts.

In those heady first years of Viennese modernism, Hevesi had held Loos at arm's length. It was not only that Loos was pointedly not a Secessionist (Hevesi tagged him correctly as a "Nichtsezessionist"); he was also wary of Loos's radical stance, his rejection of modern ornament and all that went with it.[2] Still, Hevesi had a grudging respect for Loos. He wrote of Loos's spare, "nihilistic" interior for the Café Museum, describing it as "appetitlich, logisch, praktisch" (appealing, logical, and practical)–words of a certain regard, if not exactly unabashed praise.[3]

After that time, Hevesi kept his eye on Loos, watching to see whether Loos's early promise might amount to something he could support. It was a sensible stance. Loos's later celebrity conceals an important truth about his *Werdegang*, his

Fig. 1| Ludwig Hevesi, 1905.
Fig. 2| Adolf Loos, caricature by Carl Leopold Hollitzer, with an inscription from Peter Altenberg, 1908.

becoming. He was thirty-six years old at the time that Hevesi's piece appeared and not yet as famous, or infamous, as he would be in later years (fig. 2). He had first found notice in 1898 with his splendidly written—and frequently cranky—essays about the Imperial Jubilee Exhibition, which appeared weekly that spring, summer, and fall in the *Neue Freie Presse,* the city's leading newspaper. And he had caused a stir when the Café Museum opened its doors in April 1899. Mostly, though, he had faded in and out of the front lines of the design debates. Nearly all of Loos's works were for shops or apartments for private clients; beyond these clients' customers and acquaintances, he would likely not have been more than a distant catchword. To the extent that he did draw notice, most took his name to be synonymous with a decidedly wide-eyed radicalism.

Only one longer portrait of Loos appeared before Hevesi wrote his piece for the *Fremden-Blatt.* It was published in *Innen-Dekoration,* a German journal devoted to interiors and read mostly by design professionals. Its author was Wilhelm Schölermann, a German art historian who had served for a time as the editor of *Ver Sacrum,* the Viennese Secessionists' little magazine.

Schölermann's article was an omnibus review of the recent efforts of Vienna's interior designers. It stands out now because it was one of the first pieces to record a signal moment in Viennese modernism: the shift, beginning around 1901, away from the ornamental exercises of the early Jugendstil toward to a new purism, the banishment of ornament in favor of astringent surfaces and clear lines. "This movement," Schölermann notes, "began with a new ornament in [the form of a] 'stylized linearization.'"[4] What followed, he describes, was a quick turn away from ornament itself. The central figure in this redirection, he emphasizes, was Loos. "I have known and followed the steadfast work, the quiet actions of this man, who is essentially the antipode of the Secession and has very little that is Viennese about him. His style is logic made material. His aesthetic is the renouncement of everything that is unnecessary. Functional form [*Zweckform*] for him is the highest commandment of beauty."[5]

Even more, Schölermann's portrayal is a clarion statement of Loos's attitude toward ornament: "Loos loathes ornament. He describes himself as an *Ornament-killer* [Schölermann's word]. He also wants to hear nothing about how handcraft should be reformed by artists."[6]

One would be hard pressed to say that more directly. Schölermann picked up something else about Loos, something others missed or chose to ignore. Loos's anti-ornament crusade was founded on an ethical and moral basis. Loos, he tells his readers, repudiated modern ornament because it was wasteful; Loos attacked those making new ornament because they were out of step with the times.

Hevesi knew all this, of course. In a review written not long before his feature on Loos appeared, he refers to a particular furniture ensemble as "à la Loos." It was an acknowledgment of its startling simplicity and its strict underlying logic.[7]

Little else about Loos appeared in Vienna's newspapers or journals around the time of Hevesi's portrait. One exception was a curious notice in the daily *Neues Wiener Tagblatt*, from January 30, 1907. It was a brief report concerning the murder of one Dr. Charles Townsend in New York. The paper had picked up the story because Townsend had studied medicine in Vienna in the early 1890s. Several people remembered him and his wife from that time. Loos, the article mentions in passing, had visited Townsend on Staten Island in 1893 during his time in America.[8]

What is telling here is that the reporter thought this meeting with Townsend worth mentioning. Loos is identified as the "Architekt Adolf Loos"—enough to suggest that a reader might be familiar with him.

There was another mention of Loos in the newspapers that April, in a classified advertisement, offering an apartment for either sale or rent adjacent to Arenberg Park. It pointedly noted that the design was Loos's—implying that his name had a certain caché.[9]

Loos, however, sought greater notice. It was he who approached Hevesi about writing the piece in the *Fremden-Blatt*, not the other way around.[10] Hevesi admits in his feature that he had waited a long time—since he reviewed the finished Café Museum—to write anything longer about Loos. He reveals that before he started to pen the piece, Loos had taken him on a tour of his interiors, including many of the private apartments. There is evidence, too, that he spoke extensively with Loos—he may even have formally interviewed him—since he cites Loos several times at length.

What is apparent to anyone who has spent time reading Loos's essays is that Hevesi presents a crisply accurate picture of his thought. He seems to have been quite taken with Loos's blunt assertions. Hevesi quotes Loos as saying, "To spend time creating ornament these days, one has to have a very average mind; a more highly organized brain isn't making ornament these days, it has better things to do."[11] Hevesi doubtless published this statement for its shock value. But he clearly enjoyed Loos's outlandishness. Also, remarkably, Hevesi gives us a rare glimpse of Loos's distinctive manner of speaking—his almost incessant spewing out of words and ideas. He writes with merriment about Loos's tendency to prattle on in lengthy monologues, "in two-centimeter-long blocks of text; not a period anywhere, just dashes."[12]

Hevesi's article is not long—about a dozen paragraphs, the standard length of a feuilleton at the time. He managed to pack almost everything that mattered about Loos into those lines: Loos's rejection of ornament, his contrariness, his distance from—and pronounced antipathy for—Hoffmann, Olbrich, and the other Secessionists, his devotion to handcraft and craftspeople. He also picks up on a key point not a few of Loos's enemies and even some of his supporters failed to grasp: Loos's belief that any manifestation of design was part of a longer cultural evolution, that it made no sense to exclude objects or forms from the past if they still had relevance. "Thus, anything that is genuine will fit [into his interiors]. An old piano with its plain craftsmanship."[13] Hevesi notes, too, with some surprise, that Loos didn't design his own chairs. He "relies on replicas of the English originals" because they are "right" and "eternal."[14]

The significance of Hevesi's portrait rests not only with its early and insightful assessment of Loos and his ideas. The essential lines come at the end: "Up to now Loos has almost never appeared in the illustrated art journals. There is a reason for that. His rooms look like nothing in photographs. 'The people who dwell within would not know them.'"[15] In other words, if you want to appreciate Loos's interiors, you must see them in person.

Fig. 3| Adolf Loos, *Wohnungswanderungen*, Vienna, 1907. Brochure.

ZWEITER TAG

VIII. Wickenburggasse 24, Mezzanin, Wohnung des Dr. T.

Speisezimmer Kirsche, Ordinationszimmer Mahagoni, Schlafzimmer in Battist rayée (Damenblusenstoff). Nach dem in der »Kunst« erschienenen Schlafzimmer meiner Frau.

IX. Alserstraße 22, I. Stock, Wohnung des Dr. Sch. (Kein Aufzug.)

Vorzimmer weißer Lack, Speisezimmer braungebeiztes Eichenholz, japanische Tapete: grass cloth (aus Grass gewoben), Sitzzimmer weißer Lack, alter Kamin.

IX. Alserstraße 53, II. Stock, Wohnung des Dr. H. (Kein Aufzug.)

Speisezimmer. Soll auch als Besuchszimmer verwendet werden. Häßlicher Ofen mit großer Uhr verbaut. Als Blumenständer alt-italienischer Trog. (Abguß.) Dunkel gebeizte Eiche. Arbeitszimmer unfertig, zum Vergrößern eingerichtet. Schlafzimmer in Ahorn.

Fig. 4| Adolf Loos, *Wohnungswanderungen*, "Zweiter Tag."

This is precisely what Loos had in mind. His invitation to Hevesi to tour the shops and apartments was part of a plan he had been hatching for some time: to conduct a public tour of his interiors.[16]

Loos placed notices in several newspapers, and he had a small brochure printed (figs. 3, 4). The announced dates for the event were December 10 and 11, 1907. Tickets for the self-guided tour were available at two of Loos's commercial spaces, the Goldman & Salatsch tailor salon (the original one on the Graben) and the Sigmund Steiner Decorative Feather shop. Loos had recently completed the latter in the fashionable Kärntner Straße. Hevesi had singled out the design in his piece as an especially representative example of Loos's ideas.[17]

The tickets for the tour were priced at twenty kronen for a party of two, more than one hundred dollars today. (The money, according to the brochure, was to go to a "good cause.") The high admission fee was evidently an effort to limit the number of visitors.

The program included the two shops and twelve private residences:

First Day 10 December 1907
1., Graben 20: Goldman & Salatsch tailor shop and the apartment of Emanuel Aufricht and his wife Berta in the same building.
1., Kärntner Straße 33, Sigmund Steiner Shop
4., Schleifmühlgasse 2, apartment of Annie Wagner-Wünsch
1., Openring 13, dining room in the apartment of Leopold Langer
1., Elisabethstraße 15, gentleman's room in the apartment of Dr. Alfred Sobotka
1., Falkestraße 6, music room in the apartment of Georg and Else Weiss
4., Wohllebengasse 19, apartment of Gustav and Marie Turnowsky
1., Nibelungengasse 13, apartment of Rudolf Kraus

Second Day 11 December 1907
8., Wickenburggasse 24, apartment of Dr. Rudolf Türkel
9., Alserstraße 22, apartment of Dr. Ludwig and Clothilde Schweiger
9., Alserstraße 53, apartment of Dr. Hugo Haberfeld
8., Josefstädter Straße 68, apartment of Hermann and Eugenie Schwarzwald
8., Josefstädter Straße 73, apartment of Dr. Viktor Groser
1., Bellariastraße 4, apartment of Arthur and Leonie Friedmann

The shops were scheduled for visitation on the first day. But they were in fact available for viewing both days, a Tuesday and Wednesday, because they were open for regular business.[18] Oddly, and for reasons never explained, Loos's own apartment

Fig. 5| Adolf Loos, apartment of Rudolf Kraus, Vienna 1., Nibelungengasse 13, 1907.
Fig. 6| Adolf Loos, apartment of Dr. Hermann and Dr. Eugenie Schwarzwald, Vienna 8., Josefstädter Straße 68, 1905, altered in 1909.
Fig. 7| Adolf Loos, "Wohnungs-Moden," *Frankfurter Zeitung*, Zweites Morgenblatt, 8 December 1907.

Feuilleton.

Wohnungs-Moden.

Von **Adolf Loos** (Wien).*)

Man spricht seit zwei Jahren von einem Bankerott der modernen Wohnungseinrichtungen. Man spricht davon, daß man wieder zu den alten Stilen zurückkehren solle. Und als letztes Heilmittel wird Biedermeyer verschrieben. In Deutschland hieß die moderne Bewegung Jugendstil. Bei uns Sezession. Beide Bezeichnungen sind Schimpfwörter geworden. Es sind bald zehn Jahre her, daß ich in einer Reihe von Artikeln vor diesen beiden Stilarten warnte. Ich sagte damals: Man möge sich weder in einer alten, noch in einer der neuen Stilarten einrichten, sondern modern. Mit meiner Ansicht blieb ich damals in der Minorität. In einer sehr kleinen Minorität sogar: Es war die Minoritätszahl eins. Unsere modernen Erzeugnisse wurden sowohl von den Künstlern, als auch von den staatlichen Behörden mit Geringschätzung behandelt. Ich verwies darauf, daß es doch gar nicht notwendig sei, den Stil unserer Zeit erst zu konstruieren, da wir ihn doch schon besitzen. Unsere Maschinen, unsere Kleidung, unsere Wagen und Pferdegeschirre, unsere Glas- und Metallwaren und alles, alles, was einer unzeitgemäßen Verballhornung durch die Architekten entgangen war, war modern. Gewiß, die Tischlerarbeit war den Architekten seit 50 Jahren in Bausch und Bogen ausgeliefert. Es galt daher, sie von den Architektenwitzen und Kinkerlitzen zu befreien. Dann würde uns für die moderne Wohnungseinrichtung nichts mehr fehlen.

on Bösendorferstraße, completed in 1903, was not on the program. Loos also did not attend any of the viewings. In fact, he was not present at all. He and his then partner, the English dancer Bessie Bruce, were vacationing in Semmering, south of Vienna, in the Alps.[19]

Loos's biographers Burkhardt Rukschcio and Roland Schachel speculate that he excluded himself and his own residence because he wanted to remove himself from the center of attention.[20] The true reasons, however, might be different. The Bösendorferstraße apartment may not have been in the best condition. Loos's first wife, Lina (née Obertimpfler), had moved out two years before. Later photographs show it in considerable disarray. And Loos may not have attended because he feared criticism and did not want to feel the sting of attacks.

It is not known how many people took the tour. Given the hefty admission cost—and the modest size of the apartments—it could not have been a large number. One of the few known visitors was Loos's friend, the writer and poet Richard Schaukal.[21]

The apartments and the two shops Loos included in the tour shared some common characteristics. All been completed within eight or nine years—since the time Loos began designing interiors in Vienna. The spaces were also owned by clients who in every case were befriended with Loos or, at least, connected to him in some way. They shared a cohesive look: Loos had used the same suppliers and craftspeople, and, despite the passage of time, he had hardly altered his design strategies (figs. 5, 6).

To set the stage for the event—and make his intentions clear—Loos published a short polemic in the *Frankfurter Zeitung* (fig. 7). It appeared on December 8, two days before the tours were set to start.[22]

It is unclear why Loos chose not to publish the piece in a Viennese newspaper. It may have been, as Rukschcio and Schachel write, that Loos wanted to limit his audience. Another explanation, however, would be more revealing of his position in Vienna. It is quite possible that none of the local papers wanted to be associated with Loos's contrarian views. Even the editors of the *Frankfurter Zeitung*, although choosing to publish Loos's piece, voiced their reservations. At the bottom of the essay's first column, which appeared in the feuilleton section on page one, was a short statement from the editors pointedly distancing themselves from some of Loos's ideas: "Adolf Loos has rendered great service to the movement for modern arts and crafts and the modern design of our homes. We therefore gladly give space to his remarks without adopting them in all points."[23]

Loos's text gave the editors ample cause for concern. The text is so poignant and exceptional that it is worth quoting at length. (The full piece, in German, is in the appendix.)

> For the past two years, people have been talking about the bankruptcy of modern domestic design. They talk about the need to return to the old styles.

And most recently, the Biedermeier is being prescribed as the remedy. In Germany, the modern movement was called Jugendstil. In our country, it was called Secession. Both terms have become pejoratives. It is now nearly ten years ago that I warned against these two styles in a series of essays. At that time, I said that one should not design spaces in either one of the old or the new styles, but rather in a modern one. With my opinion, I remained at that time in the minority. In a very small minority. A minority of one. Our modern products were treated with contempt both by the artists and by the state authorities. I pointed out that it was not necessary to construct the style of our time, since we already had it. Our machines, our clothes, our carriages and harnesses, our glass and metal goods, and everything else that has escaped the architect's untimely corruption, was modern. Certainly, carpentry had been at the mercy of architects for fifty years. Therefore, it was necessary to free it from the architects' jests and bits and bobs [*Architekten-witzen und Kinkerlitzen*]. Then, we could no longer lack anything for modern home furnishings.

The way to it was very simple. Certain products of the carpenter, the woodworker had escaped the architect. Now we had to collect them and apply their forms to similar cases. There were the cassettes that the piccolo carried around in the Viennese restaurants to serve the cigars. There were ice chests for "frozen food" in the Viennese coffee houses. There were glass display cases in the commercial interior design industry. There were fittings, also around everywhere, key plates used in the manufacture of suitcases. And even how wall paneling would have evolved, one could learn: through the water closets, which had such wall paneling to board up the water box and the wall.

Now, you had modern joinery. This carpenter's work lacked that which was a prerequisite for the architect's cooperation: ornament. Since the old furniture had carved or inlaid ornaments and profiles, but the modern carpenter cannot draw any, the architect imposed himself. The carpenter cannot do it because he is a modern man. The architect could and can because he is an unfashionable man. Because—I also claimed this ten years ago—a modern man is no longer capable of producing an ornament. The modern products of our culture have no ornament. Suitcase and leather workers, tailors, electricians, machine manufacturers do not apply ornament. Only people who were born in the present, but in fact live in an earlier century, women, the rural population, the Orientals (the Japanese included) and mutilated brains like those of the tile and wallpaper pattern draftsmen still produce a new ornament of equal value to the old one.

The inability of our culture to create a new ornament is its greatness. The evolution of mankind goes hand in hand with the removal of ornament from the object of daily use. Let our applied artists—out of an instinct for self-preservation—object as they want. For the cultured man, a non-tattooed face

> is more beautiful than a tattooed one, even if the tattoo comes from Kolo Moser himself. And the cultured man wants to know that not only his skin, but also his book covers, or his bedside cabinet, are protected from the Indian-ornamental-rage of our state-employed cultural barbarians.
>
> Ornament that does not spring organically from the human soul, as in old masters or the new Oriental, is worthless. Worthless, lost work, wasted material. And this worthlessness increases day by day. Objects of daily use that seemed valuable to buyers just five years ago can now barely fetch a tenth of their purchase price at the Dorotheum. Make no mistake about it: objects produced according to today's unsophisticated and therefore outmoded, i.e., unfashionable direction, will meet the same fate in a few years.
>
> We should strive to create lasting values.

It is hardly surprising, then, given the stridency of Loos's statements, that the editors of the *Frankfurter Zeitung* sought to distance themselves. Hardly anyone involved in any way with the new design emerges unscathed—except, of course, Loos's beloved craftspeople.

What is arresting for anyone conversant with Loos's published writings is how much this essay anticipates his "Ornament und Verbrechen" (Ornament and crime), written, as we now know, in late 1909 or early 1910.[24] Almost all the essential ingredients are already developed, including Loos's key assertation: "Evolution der Menschheit geht Hand in Hand mit dem Entfernen des Ornamentes aus dem Gebrauchs-gegenstande" (the evolution of humanity goes hand in hand with the removal of ornament from the object of daily use), stated nearly verbatim in "Ornament und Verbrechen."[25]

The full text of Loos's piece was reproduced in the "Wohnungswanderungen" guide. He certainly wrote that version first. What appeared in the newspaper was a condensation of the full essay, without most of the five final paragraphs—about a third of the entire text. Almost surely, it was the paper's editors who shortened it. The reason they likely did so was not for lack of space, but because Loos in this section takes direct aim at his opponents, mentioning by name Olbrich, Hoffmann, and Henry van de Velde.

The remainder of the guide was a list of the apartments and other interiors one could visit, along with brief descriptions. In the case of the Turnowsky Apartment, Loos writes: "Vestibule not by me. Gentleman's room in mahogany, with existing furniture," and so on.[26] The descriptions are useful nowadays in that they help us understand precisely what was Loos's work and what was existing or not his design. But the almost deadpan tone conceals the radical cast of Loos's approach to his designs.

Design is not the correct word: *assembly* would be more accurate. Loos was essentially selecting and combining the furnishings and other fittings. A few pieces were from his hand—that is, they were "designed" by him—but the aggregate was in the best sense a compilation. There is nonetheless an evident consistency to what he was doing: he selected things that were in his view good design, whether new or old, and he made space for the objects that the clients already had, whether good or bad. Everything he arranged in such a way to facilitate the patterns of daily life—a Viennese bourgeois lifestyle, it should be underscored. Often, the furnishings and other objects are arranged casually. Only some larger pieces he intended to be fixed in place; and many things, he foresaw, could be readily traded out, replaced, or moved.

At the end of the guide, Loos made a few additional comments, thanking his clients and noting the names of his makers and suppliers. The final paragraph, however, stands out: "I will only execute apartments for those clients, who are deeply drawn to [what I do]. Snobs are excluded. The rooms will not be published in the art periodicals, and there will be no more such tours."[27]

Loos kept his word. He never again mounted a tour—or any public exhibition—of his interiors.

If Loos hoped that the event would bring him into the spotlight, he was sadly mistaken. For the next two years, he remained on the sidelines.

His still-marginal status is revealed in the visit of the young Charles Edouard Jeanneret—the future Le Corbusier—to Vienna. The twenty-year-old Jeanneret arrived in the fall of 1907, perhaps as early as September. He stayed for several months. He was a keen observer, noting the salient examples of Viennese modernism. We know from his writings that he was much taken with Hoffmann's designs for the Wiener Werkstätte; he even pondered asking Hoffmann for a position. Jeanneret may have been in the city when the tour of Loos's interiors was taking place. Yet in the account of his travels, he failed to mention Loos even once.[28]

Loos did figure prominently in an essay written in mid-December 1907 by socialite Berta Zuckerkandl, who, like Hevesi, was one of the foremost art critics of the day. Zuckerkandl published a lengthy feuilleton in the *Wiener Allgemeine Zeitung* extolling the achievements of Vienna's decorative artists, in particular Hoffmann and Moser and their designs for the Wiener Werkstätte. She writes of Loos's efforts to introduce a "sachlich" (literally "objective," but here "purist") Viennese style, describing his interiors for the Café Museum as his "characteristic protest against the 'ornamental plunder' of 'florets, waves and bows,'" which, in her words, constituted a "false Secession."[29]

We have no reaction from Loos's side to this. But the words "false Secession" must have rung in his ears. Zuckerkandl was referring to the mountains of kitsch that issued from Vienna's less august factories and workshops, the endless glut of picture frames, mirrors, glasses, porcelain, and the like that had flooded the market with their pale imitations of the Jugendstil, not the products of Hoffmann and the other leaders of the movement. Loos must have viewed it differently. The "false Secession," like the Secession itself, in his eyes was the same misguided response to the problem of how to craft a modern design. It mattered not a whit to him whether these products stemmed from Hoffmann and the consummate makers of the Wiener Werkstätte or manufacturers of shoddy goods in the *Vorstädte*.

Loos spent time in London that winter with Bessie Bruce.[30] We know nothing of what he did or saw, but the visit (his second to the city) must have only reinforced his abiding admiration for English design and taste.

The next crucial moment for Loos came in July 1908. He learned that a meeting was to take place in Munich, the stated purpose of which was the first plenary gathering of a new organization, the Deutscher (or German) Werkbund. The group had been officially founded on October 6, 1907. The inaugural meeting was scheduled for July 11 and 12, 1908, at the tony Hotel Vier Jahreszeiten.

The Werkbund had been conceived as an association of artists, architects, and designers. Its stated purpose—at least at first—was to establish a partnership of product manufacturers with design professionals to improve the competitiveness of German companies in the world marketplace. Based on his subsequent statements, Loos must have suspected that the other—concealed—agenda of the *Werkbündler* was to define a specific stylistic direction for modernism, an idea for which he had not the least bit of sympathy.

Loos was not the only Viennese modernist to attend the meeting. Among the delegates were Hoffmann, Klimt, Fritz Wärndorfer (the textile manufacturer who was bankrolling the Wiener Werkstätte), and the designers Bertold Löffler, Otto Prutscher, and Carl Witzmann.[31] Loos, who had not been invited, went "as an interested person."[32]

At first, Loos observed the proceedings quietly. Only on the second day, at the prompting of Josef Frank, then an architecture student at the Technische Hochschule, did he attempt to speak. But he was prevented from doing so because he was not a member of the organization.[33]

Loos, however, was not content to hold his silence. Shortly after returning to Vienna, he published a scathing piece on the Werkbund and its aims in the Munich-based publication *März*.

The little journal was edited by four prominent figures in the Munich avant-garde, Ludwig Thoma, Hermann Hesse, Albert Langen, and Hans Fischer (who published under the pseudonym Kurt Aram). It billed itself as an alternative to *Simplicissimus*, which was closely associated with the Jugendstil and its makers. This may explain Loos's choice of this particular publication.

He titled his essay "Die Überflüssigen" (The superfluous ones). The phrase referred to his belief that modernism required no standing organization to promote it, that the Werkbund was an assault on a true modernism (which had already arisen in the crafts), and that the efforts of the "designers" were at best unnecessary, at worst injurious to the whole enterprise. Loos was especially critical of some of the products of this kind of thinking—and its consequences:

> The assault on our modern culture on the part of these "artists," so completely lacking in culture, has been repudiated. The inkwells (a rocky cleft with two nymphs), the candlesticks (a girl holding a jug in which the candle rests), the furniture (the bedside tables are small drums, the sideboard a large drum with a jigsaw cutout of an oak tree clutching it in its splayed branches) stayed on the store shelf. And if someone does buy this stuff, two years hence he is ashamed of having it in his possession. The art was a failure. But they had made their presence felt, and they had to make a living. So, they hit on the ploy of saying that our culture needed their help.[34]

Loos was adamant that attempting to "reframe" design made no sense, since modernity was fundamentally an expression of culture and could not be imposed. His parting shot at the end of the essay is pointed and, as so often the case with Loos, mordantly amusing: "What we need is a 'cabinetmakers' culture' [i.e., one arising directly from the efforts of craftspeople], and were the applied artists to return to painting pictures or sweeping the streets, we would have one."[35]

Thoma and Hesse, *März*'s lead editors, were only too happy to support Loos's effort because they sympathized with his message. They were mindful, though, that Loos, as they wrote in a short editorial on the issue's last page, was likely "only familiar to a small number of our readers," and that his uncompromising stance required explanation—and justification. Loos's interiors, they added, were helping Vienna to move toward a "stricter and more serious style" (*strengeren und ernsteren Stil*) and were having their impact on the "Wiener Schule" (Viennese School) and in Germany. Consequently, they asked Loos to write a series of additional articles for the journal.[36]

Loos agreed. He followed "Die Überflüssigen" with two other essays.[37] But the controversy Loos had helped to ignite did not die down.[38] It would rage over the next two years and culminate in one of the signal moments in the march of early modernism.

Chapter 2

The Imperatives of the Past and Present

The inaugural meeting of the German Werkbund in Munich was not the sole event of great import for the Viennese modernists in the summer of 1908. On June 1, a vast exhibition of new art, architecture, and design—called simply Kunstschau, or Art Show, 1908—opened on the grounds of the future Konzerthaus in the city's third district. It was conceived in part as one of the many events and festivities marking the sixtieth anniversary of the reign of Emperor Franz Joseph I. Far more, though, it was an effort at artistic redefinition. Its organizers, some fifteen leading artists, architects, and designers, including Klimt, Hoffmann, Moser, Carl Moll, Alfred Roller, Carl Otto Czeschka, and Otto Prutscher, all of whom were aligned with the Klimtgruppe (those who had joined Klimt when he quit the Vienna Secession in 1905), were intent upon promoting a new and more advanced vision of modernism.

In 1907, the group had formed a committee to plan their exhibition, electing Klimt as president. Without a suitable building—Olbrich's Secession building had remained in the hands of the original organization—they decided to construct their own temporary exhibition hall. Hoffmann was given the task of designing it. He contrived a large wooden and stucco structure, of approximately 6,500 square meters, with fifty-four exhibition rooms, a café, courtyard, outdoor theater, and gardens.[39]

The centerpiece of the exhibition was the Klimt Room housing sixteen of his paintings, including *The Kiss* and the portraits of Margarethe Stonborough-Wittgenstein and Adele Bloch-Bauer. Some 170 other artists took part, many of them students at the Vienna Akademie der bildenden Künste, the Kunstgewerbeschule, or the Wiener Frauenakademie.[40]

Klimt, as intended, was the star of the event. But the whole, seen from today's vantage, was a delineation of the past, present, and future of the new art and design in Central Europe. The past—more precisely, the recent past—was on display in the works of the late Impressionists (Carl Moll, for instance) and the Symbolists (Adolf Hölzel). Most of the exhibition, however, resounded in the visual tones of the lively present, in the paintings of Klimt, of course, but also those of Broncia Koller-Pinell, and the designs of Moser, Czeschka, Roller, and others. There were also a few glances into the future, in the contributions of the young artists Oskar Kokoschka and František Kupka.

Very much of the design work on display—the decorative and graphic arts—replicated what might be cast as the "geometricized Jugendstil," the form canon that had replaced the early Viennese reliance on natural forms. The Secessionists relied on squares, circles, and triangles (and their serial reproduction), which they presented not only as abstractions of the natural world but also as standalone expressions, as a new ornamental language. Already by 1903, this modus—first announced by Hoffmann and Moser just after the turn of the century—had become the definition of Viennese modernism *tout court*, and it would remain so for another five or six years.

Hoffmann was the other leading light of the Kunstschau 1908 (fig. 8). He was thirty-seven years old that summer, at the height of his powers. His fame, tightly bound up with his designs for the Wiener Werkstätte, now extended well beyond Vienna (fig. 9, 10). The exhibition was hardly his coming-out, but the sundry ensembles and pieces (many made by the Werkstätte's consummate artisans) spoke in the idiom of a gleaming modernity.

Hoffmann's temporary building appeared as a pleasure palace, a *Lustschloss*, from the age of Maria Theresia (fig. 11). Despite its simple, even plain surfaces, it represented a decided shift for him. Embedded in the building and its spaces were many moments that stated a very different notion of modernism and its meanings. Most notable was Hoffmann's newfound interest in a purified classicism. After pushing toward a radical reductivism in his work, he had begun, around 1906, to consider how the classical tradition might be modernized. His masterwork in his newly invented idiom was the Palais Stoclet in Brussels, a premonitory glance toward what would become the "art deco" of the 1920s and 1930s.

The Kunstschau building was distinctly pared down by comparison, a compromise between the elementary geometry of Hoffmann's earlier style and a new—or renewed—thinking about the essence of classical form. The smoking

room, set in the model "country house" that stood adjacent to the main pavilion, drew on all these influences—and another one: the sensibilities and sinuous lines of the Rococo (fig. 12). Many of Hoffmann's interiors, however, spoke in a different language, a melding of Biedermeier classicism and his own fertile imagination (fig. 13).

The Biedermeier revival, which was in full motion by 1908, was an obvious source for Hoffmann (as it was for many other designers in Central Europe at the time).[41] What set his interiors apart was his growing engagement with history as a whole. For an architect and designer who had begun his education when historicism was still ascendant, this was perhaps not an unexpected turn. Novel,

Fig. 8| Josef Hoffmann, 1903.

Fig. 9| Wiener Werkstätte showroom, Vienna 7., Neustiftgasse 32–34, ca. 1904–5.

Fig. 10| Wiener Werkstätte showroom, Vienna 7., Neustiftgasse 32–34, ca. 1905.

Fig. 11| Josef Hoffmann, reception hall, seen from the garden side, Kunstschau 1908, Vienna.

Fig. 12| Josef Hoffmann, smoking room (Room 44), Kunstschau 1908, Vienna.
Fig. 13| Josef Hoffmann, children's bedroom in white, Kunstschau 1908, Vienna.

though, for Hoffmann was a willingness to suspend the headlong search for simplicity and reengage what had only recently been cast off: the full weight of the European past.

This seeming retrenchment owed something to the fact that Hoffmann and others in Vienna feared that they might have thrown off tradition too hastily. Even more, Hoffmann saw the inherent possibilities in a creative rapprochement with history—that it might be possible to articulate modernity with a greater cultural sophistication, one that was additive rather than exclusionary.

But what Hoffmann was exploring (and would do for the remainder of his long career) was not merely an extension of the old historicism. He appended a new set of tactics, new ways of mining the past. In the most direct terms, he was moving away from any kind of copying, relying instead on creative "reinvention." Or, put differently, he was making historical forms and references that were somehow recognizable, but which had never previously existed.

Perhaps the most immediate example of this design tactic is a motif he used often in the years before the Great War, the fluting from a classical column that is converted into "surface." He did so, for instance, in the façade of the Austrian pavilion at the 1914 Werkbund exhibition, wrapping it in what reads as a flattened column (fig. 14). The idea was not unprecedented—even the Greek architects of the Hellenistic period had made something of the sort, disassembling classical elements and shifting them in scale or altering the syntax of their placement. In the same way, Michelangelo and the other Italian Mannerists had also experimented freely with the classical form canon, in the process devising a stylistic idiom that was uniquely theirs.

Hoffmann, though, went further. He retained the legibility of the form: the fluting still reads as fluting. That much is unmistakable. Yet its logic is altered to such a degree that neither its tectonic nor its iconological sense is retained. The "column" is not a "carrying" element; it no longer represents reeded bundles or natural striations. It has become pattern.

In his works of the late prewar period, Hoffmann also elides the traditional separation between architecture and the decorative arts. The same motif of extended fluting appears in his table legs and sideboards. The façades of his buildings and furnishings were nearly identical. Only their scale is different.

Eduard F. Sekler, who produced the most extensive study of Hoffmann's architectural oeuvre, noted one other important change in Hoffmann's work around the time of the Kunstschau 1908: a new pluralism. Hoffmann's "artistic point of departure," he writes, "was already very different" from what it "had been in earlier years. For [him and the other] adherents of the 'Moderne' no simple unified position existed anymore; the time of *Ver Sacrum* [i.e., the "sacred spring," the apex of the Secessionists' efforts] was over."[42]

Hoffmann would never again subscribe to the idea that modernism should have a specific stylistic definition. In decided contrast to most other European modernists, he also never abandoned his belief that history could be included in the architecture and design of the present.

Hoffmann's rejection of the belief that modernism represented a caesura, a wholesale leaving of the past, was shared by most of the other Viennese modernists. The faith in cultural continuity, in a usable past, would become one of the core tenets of the *Wiener Moderne* for the next three decades. But the Viennese drew quite different, and often competing, conclusions from this idea. The full construct of what was truly past and what still defined the present became the battlefield on which many of their most concerted assaults took place.

In August 1908, not long after his diatribe against the German Werkbund appeared, Loos published a second essay in *März*. "Lob der Gegenwart" (In praise of the present) is a curious response to the question what was—or should be—modern, for it deals solely with the issue of fashion. The basic premise is that to be truly modern one should dress in a modern way. It was not an unfamiliar point for Loos; he had previously shown much interest in the appropriateness of clothes and dressing, both for men and for women. Yet the essay also functions as an extended metaphor: it can be read as a statement about *how* one should live in the modern age.

It begins, as is so often the case with Loos, with a seemingly modest assertion: "If I think about the previous millennia and ask myself, in which age I might have most wanted to live, I say to myself: in the present one. Oh, I know at times it was a pleasure to be alive. Some epochs have this advantage, others another one. And perhaps one lived in every time more happily than in this one. But in no other time could one go around so beautifully, well, and practically dressed as today."[43] Loos goes on to point out the impracticality of formal dress throughout the ages, and how the English, with their sedate and sensible clothing, had come to rule the world.

Loos's point here is not about clothing at all—or only tangentially so. He is after a much more central idea: that life in the modern age is far less about appearance than it is about living freely and prospering. What enables us to advance as a people and find contentment in life is closely bound up with reality and utility.

Loos picked up this theme again in his third essay for *März*, which appeared a short time later. He titled it "Kultur" (Culture). It takes a similarly oblique approach to the question of what is right for the present, probing various cultural norms, especially in England and Germany, in a broad way. Loos's answer was the same: that the essence of modernity rests with practicality. His hero is the American worker, "the man in overalls," who had "conquered the world."[44]

Neither of these essays responds directly to the challenge that Hoffmann was posing that summer in his designs for the Kunstschau. It was all well and good for Loos to insist on the useful and the "functional." But he never answers the deeper question: What *form* should the new interior take?

Fig. 14| Josef Hoffmann, Austrian Pavilion at the 1914 Werkbund exhibition, Cologne.

His reply came in a third essay, also apparently written in 1908 but not published until many years later.

From all we know, Loos wrote "Kulturentartung" (Cultural degeneration) for *März*.[45] Why it did not appear in the journal is unknown. It is possible that the editors deemed it too controversial. (It should be said, though, that "Die Überflüssigen" was nearly as strident.) Perhaps it was because Loos this time named more names and offered more pointed criticism. Whatever the case, "Kulturentartung" picks up the argument Loos was making in his first *März* essay, articulating much more bluntly his alternative vision of modernism and its expression. In so doing, he laid down the basis of the design debate that would echo for the next several years.

At the outset, Loos again issues his assertion that the German Werkbund was wholly misguided in its aims: "The members of this organization are people, who are attempting to replace our present-day culture with another one. Why they are doing this, I don't know. But I know that they will not succeed. No one has ever put his plump hand in the spokes of the spinning wheel of time without having it torn off."[46] The culture of the present was already firmly established, Loos insists, for he saw it expressed in the everyday products of ordinary craftspeople: "We have our culture, our forms in which our lives play out, our objects of daily use, which make this life possible. No person, no organization designed our wardrobes, our cigarette cases, our pieces of jewelry. Our time designed them for us. They change from year to year, from day to day, from hour to hour. Because from hour to hour we ourselves change, our views, our habits. And through this action our culture changes."[47] The fundamental flaw in the Werkbund program, Loos asserts, is a confusion of cause and effect. "We do not sit in a certain way because the cabinetmaker made the chair in a certain way, but because we want to sit in a certain way."[48]

It is a brilliant but straightforward argument. Forms evolve as we do, as our culture does. It makes no sense to decree what those forms should be or how they should be constituted. To do so is to subvert the natural progress of development.

Later historians have pointed to nineteenth-century ideas of evolution (biological or cultural, Darwin or Spencer) as the origins for Loos's design philosophy. The source, however, might be nearer at hand, in Alois Riegl's notion of the *Kunstwollen*, or a "will to art." Riegl had developed the idea in his book *Die spätrömische Kunst-Industrie nach den Funden in Österreich-Ungarn* (The late Roman art industry according to the finds in Austria-Hungary), in which he sought to understand how and why the appearance of art and everyday objects in the late Roman period had changed from earlier times.[49] The idea of a Kunstwollen was essentially Riegl's shorthand for how he thought cultural changes—which is to say, changes in attitudes and perceptions about life and the world—were reflected in everyday objects, and how these, in turn, shaped the look of the art of any age.

Loos likely encountered Riegl's ideas via his friend Karl Kraus, who was notably better read and from whom Loos evidently heard much about the contemporary intellectual discourse. In any case, the notion had gained currency at the time. It fit perfectly with Loos's belief that culture was primary, the artifacts of daily life secondary. These objects were mere reflections of how we live and what we believe. The "Kulturentartung," or cultural degeneration, of Loos's title refers to his conviction that artifice, the deliberate attempt to shape the look of art and our ordinary lives, was a corruption of the natural order, of the very premise of culture and ordinary cultural development.

Here the source for Loos is clear-cut: his title was a nearly exact borrowing from Max Nordau's two-volume book *Entartung* (Degeneration; 1892–93). The reference was deliberate: Loos saw in the "inappropriate" fiddlings of the *Werkbündler* the same cultural illness that Nordau diagnosed in the art and ideas of Richard Wagner, Oscar Wilde, Henrik Ibsen, Friedrich Nietzsche and others, who in his view had succumbed to a groundless aestheticism.

Culture was always the great driver of Loos's thought, of his entire worldview. That he would base his critique of the German Werkbund on his sense of cultural propriety is hardly unexpected. In a sense, what Loos writes is a restatement of similar remarks he had made in the 1898 Imperial Jubilee Exhibition essays. But he adds to these, embellishing them and modifying his assertions in light of what had taken place in the interim; namely, that the advent of the Secession and the Secessionists' efforts to invent their own form-language was destroying Austria's culture.

The novelty of "Kulturentartung" rests with the fact that he says more, especially about what he thinks are the correct forms of modern times. He makes three distinct but related statements about what he believes is right and appropriate.

The first is that what already exists, what has come from ordinary craftspeople, who are responding to the current needs of society, is inherently modern: "Can one deny that our leather goods are in the style of our time?! And our cutlery and glasses?! And our bathtubs and American washstands?! And our tools and machines?! And everything, everything, to state it once more, that has not fallen into the hands of our artists!"[50]

Loos's second premise is that objects are modern thanks not to their beauty, but rather to their appropriateness. "Are these objects beautiful? I don't ask about that. They are in the spirit of our age and therefore correct. They could not have belonged to a different time and could not have been used by another people."[51]

The third of Loos's notions of design "propriety" he states less directly. It comes out in his reference to his favorite cigarette case, which is, in his words, "smooth, slightly curved, and exactly worked."[52] It is thus simple and pure.

All these qualities Loos contrasts with the products of the Werkbündler, which he asserts are overdone, artificial, and tasteless. They are something else as well:

they are the result of a logic that is bound up with fashion, with the look of the moment. Loos rejects this effort to encapsulate the new, pointing out that such efforts never have staying power. They would soon appear dated, even silly, he proclaims. Here he cites as an example Hoffmann's interior for the Apollo Candle Factory, an early sounding of the Art Nouveau, which by 1908 had entirely lost its currency.

Loos's final statement in "Kulturentartung," however, is perhaps his most piercing of all (and likely the true reason why it was not published in *März*): that to make something modern, one had to be a fully and genuinely modern person. The strivings of the Werkbündler, he is saying (and not very quietly) belong to another age. They are not part of any authentic modern understanding. He closes with a dagger directed at his opponents: "Diese Zeiten sind schlechter als man denkt"—The times are worse than one would believe.[53]

"Kulturentartung" was a sharpening of Loos's assault on the Werkbund; the organization was not only unnecessary—surplus, as he had first asserted—it was injurious. It was rotting culture from within and, consequently, diminishing the conditions of modern living.

Loos's was not a lone voice of discord. Werner Sombart, the renowned German economist and historian, also rejected the Werkbund, albeit for a wholly different reason: he was convinced that a high culture could never evolve in the age of the machine. In his book *Kunstgewerbe und Kultur* (Applied arts and culture), published in 1908, Sombart declared that the applied arts would always remain at the beck and call of the capitalist industries, that profit, not aesthetics, would drive industrial production. The tastes of the masses would never rise to demand better design; and no organization or association he could imagine would alter that.[54]

The most penetrating rebuff, however, came from another contemporary observer, one initially very close to the Werkbund and its aims. The critic and writer Joseph August Lux had already joined and left the Werkbund by the end of 1908, likely departing before Loos had penned "Kulturentartung." Unlike Loos, Lux was put off less by the stated aims of the association than by his sense that the Werkbündler's rhetoric was superficial, lacking in deep questioning.

Lux had been the editor of *Hohe Warte* (High Watchtower), the Viennese publication that had noisily trumpeted the efforts of Olbrich, Hoffmann, Otto Wagner, and the other like-minded Austrian reformers. He would later write the first monographs on Olbrich and Wagner, along with several important early books on "industrial design."[55] Like Alfred Lichtwark, Karl Scheffler, and some other prominent German critics at the time, he also wrote—often glowingly—about the rise of a post-Jugendstil aesthetic.[56]

Lux at first supported the Werkbund.[57] He had long endorsed the call to design reform, and he had no illusions about the demise of the Jugendstil or the need to find a replacement. Still, Lux objected to the idea that the solution was merely a matter of pragmatics—that one could define "standards and norms," or *Typisierung*, as Hermann Muthesius, one of the leading lights of the Werkbund, had it. Lux countered that what was missing in this program was a "spiritualization of work," an awareness of the full meanings of modernity—that rationalism alone would never suffice to forge a valid new expression.

Lux's call for a new metaphysics issued from his conservative Catholicism. Nonetheless, he understood very clearly that the trend toward a new art of the machine was in the offing. In his book *Das neue Kunstgewerbe in Deutschland* (The new applied arts in Germany; 1908), published before his departure from the Werkbund, Lux argued that industrial production was the real matter at hand: "The artistic problem of our time rests not in applied arts, it lies with industry."[58] It was becoming evident, he wrote, that "there was nothing to expect from handworkers" in this regard; "new people were necessary" to take up the challenge.[59]

In his discussion of the new role of industry, Lux, however, does not address the question of what part historical forms and precedents still had to play in design, suggesting only that the marketplace would determine the shape of the new culture. For many at the time, though, the issue boiled down to one all-consuming question: what role should ornament have in modern design, especially in the modern interior.

Chapter 3

The Ornament Debate

The ornament problem was not a new one. The issue had arisen already in the 1830s—at the time when industrialization was only starting to alter the nature of how things were made, or buildings were built. In the initial onrush of this new way of thinking about ornament, it was a matter of how historical motifs might—or should—be taken over and recast, made "timely" and proper. The question for the first generation of historicists, who emerged a decade or so later, was slightly different, reflecting the shifting realities of the industrial age. What did it mean, for instance, to contrive a Gothic train station or plan a Greek-inspired bank building? How should the ornamental elements of these new structures be expressed? Exactly as before? Or in some alternative—and more fitting—way? And what might "fitting" mean?

The challenge became even more vexing a decade or two afterward, in the 1870s and 1880s, as the new historical eclecticism was taking hold. How might an ornamental motif be transformed—in scale, in placement, or in meaning? How could motifs from sundry times and cultures be fused together?

The rebellion against historical revivalism at the end of the 1880s brought forth a new set of imperatives. What could replace the forms of the past, what would it look like, and how might it be generated? In living, growing forms, John Ruskin, William Morris, and the other English reformers saw patterns of development that could be exploited and followed. With the simultaneous advent of the Art Nouveau, the faith in a novel expression, freed from the weight of the historical past, seemed to be the solution.

In Central Europe, in those last twenty years of the nineteenth century, the issue of ornament, its underlying logic, its making, and its use stood in high relief. The foremost designers made a concerted effort to stylize nature through methods that were partly scientific, and partly derived from an idealized and romanticized vision of the natural world.[60] This endeavor was felt most strongly in the schools of applied arts—the *Kunstgewerbeschulen*. But even in the architecture departments and building trades schools "reformative drawing" of natural shapes was part of the standard curriculum. Thus the young Loos, in 1886, while at the Staatsgewerbeschule, or trades school, in Reichenberg (now Liberec), was assigned to make a rendering of a stylized lily, a meticulous copy of a standard teaching pattern from a folio of such drawings (fig. 15).[61]

This fixation on nature and natural forms paved the way for the rise of the Jugendstil in Central Europe. The groundwork for a design idiom that broke with historical precedent and that was based on flora (mostly) and fauna (more rarely) had already been laid. The Viennese, however, were late to pick up the trend. It was in Munich, around 1892, that the new modus from France and Belgium first found acceptance (and its name, Jugendstil, from the magazine *Jugend*, or Youth). The initial stirrings of the new style in Vienna followed a few years later.

Yet the Viennese—at least the city's elite designers and architects—accomplished what their counterparts in Germany had not: they worked their way through all the possibilities of natural form (first by means of stylization; then, increasingly, through geometrization) and came to a radical position: the potential of a wholly abstracted form-language—pure, nonreferential motifs. Hoffmann's famed rectangular relief, shown at the Fourteenth Secession Exhibition in 1902, matched what El Lissitzky's Prouns would do more than a decade and a half later: make geometric abstraction the signature of modernity (fig. 16).

Loos, predictably, had none of it. He accepted neither the idea of a new form-canon issuing from vegetal motifs nor the resonant geometries that Hoffmann and Moser had invented. Loos regarded them merely as variant expressions of the same underlying error: a will to form that was affected and ran counter to any authentic development.

Loos's rejection of the Jugendstil was not his alone: Hoffmann and his followers had also come to a similar place by 1906, although for very different reasons. For them, the Jugendstil was beginning to look dated, even passé. They cast off what they had only recently embraced because it now appeared to be a dead end.

Loos, in "Ornament and Crime," finally put the matter to rest. But the piece was not the first salvo fired in the war on ornament, even for him. He had been voicing his thoughts about (and against) new ornament for more than a decade by the time

Fig. 15| Adolf Loos, "Lotusornament," student drawing from the State Trade School (K. k. Staatsgewerbeschule Reichenberg, Abteilung Baumeister), Reichenberg, dated November 5, 1886.
Fig. 16| Josef Hoffmann, plaster relief (detail), exhibited at the Fourteenth Secession Exhibition, 1902.

he sat down to write the piece. Loos's mighty barrage was more a directed counterattack than an opening assault.[62]

What had preceded it was a several-years-long discussion about modern ornament, precisely what it was, what it should consist of, and whether it was necessary at all.[63] The issue came up gradually but with increasing persistence, as the problem of what to do after the Jugendstil became more pressing. By 1907, those ponderings were coalescing into a debate.

There were several sides to this debate, pro or contra ornament, but also concerning how ornament "functioned," what precisely it should *say*, and how it should do so. Not a few of the texts published in these years dealt with the question of "tastefulness"—what (and how much) ornament was permissible and when and in what manner to apply it. One commentator at the time even argued for "plump ornament," the idea being that upscaling would reduce visual "clutter."[64] Many, on the other hand, simply argued for restraint.

The core of the debate was focused on whether ornament had any role at all in modern life. In an essay he published in *Innen-Dekoration* in 1907, Lux had asserted that the "renewal of ornament" by the reform architects and designers at the turn of the century was "the first creative accomplishment of modern art."[65] Others were not so sure.[66] More than one commentator called for the development of a new (i.e., post-Jugendstil) modern ornamental language.[67]

The central figure in the "anti-ornament" camp, at first, was not Loos but one of his friends, the poet, writer, and critic Richard Schaukal (fig. 17). Schaukal was four years younger than Loos. Like Loos, he had been born and reared in Brünn (Brno) and taken up residence in the capital; and, like Loos, he kept his distance from most of his contemporaries. He and Loos formed an unlikely bond, united mostly by their skepticism and wariness of easy answers.

A civil servant by profession, Schaukal began writing novels just after the turn of the century. His special theme was the superficiality and vapidity he saw around him in Vienna's hothouse culture. One of his early books, *Leben und Meinungen des Herrn Andreas von Balthesser* (The life and opinions of Mr. Andreas von Balthesser), bore the subtitle *eines Dandy und Dilettanten* (A dandy and dilettante). It was filled, as were most of his works of those years, with dry witticisms, caustic remarks, and pointed observations. Schaukal also became known for his penetrating—and often curmudgeonly—feuilletons that ran in various German-language newspapers and literary magazines.

He entered the ornament fray in April 1908, publishing a scathing attack on those calling for the development of modern ornament. His title for his article, which appeared in *Deutsche Kunst und Dekoration*, was "Gegen das Ornament" (Against ornament). It begins with an acerbic sentence that could have come directly from Loos's pen: "If a thinking person today, who is vexed, even saddened, by the commercialized culture of the present, asks himself why it is that the world, at least in

terms of that which is man-made, has become so very ugly and disconcerting, it will occur to him, if he has sharp eyes and a sense of the joy of beauty, what the answer is: the evil foe is ornament."[68] Schaukal disparaged ornament as "superfluous" and "purposeless"; he characterized the work of the Secessionists as a symptom of the "ornamental disease" (Ornamentkrankheit) then raging; and he reviled those who continued to make modern ornament. He held up his friend Loos as the only architect who had a clear vision of the future—one without ornament.[69]

Schaukal followed this with a portrait of Loos, published in the August issue of *Innen-Dekoration*, the sister publication of *Deutsche Kunst und Dekoration*.[70] The title itself was again telling: "Adolf Loos: Geistige Landschaft mit vereinzelter Figur im Vordergrund" (Adolf Loos: Spiritual landscape with an isolated figure in the foreground). Schaukal paints Loos as a solitary crusader against unnecessary and "forged" ornament—as an advocate for the "authentic expression of skillful handicraft."[71]

Fig. 17| Richard Schaukal, 1924. Photo by Hermann Clemens Kosel.

Schaukal also understood what many later commentators did not; namely, that Loos was not calling for a wholesale rejection of ornament, only that which was not "of the time." He writes: "Loos praises the historical, organic ornament, the lush and decadent arabesques of former times." In place of "new ornament," Loos "points cold-bloodedly at the essence of our modern materials," which he insists have a "sufficient effect" to express our "reality."[72] Schaukal also noted what was perhaps the key reason for Loos's objections to modern ornament, that it was wasteful, requiring extra labor, and it thus ate at the profit of those forced to make it.

The German critic Wilhelm Michel responded to Schaukal in the July 1909 issue of *Innen-Dekoration*, presenting a spirited defense of traditional architectural ornament, but agreeing with Schaukal that the Secessionists' tendency to divorce ornament from the logic of materials and structure—in Michel's words, the "kulturlose Emanzipierung des Ornaments" (uncultured emancipation of ornament)—had resulted in a mounting loss of faith in ornamental design. He suggested, however, that this development might have had a positive impact: "In all likelihood, the historic verdict of the future will be that the Jugendstil did achieve something positive: at least it possessed the will to forge something creatively new. It was destructive and it generated new possibilities—though the latter was only an indirect byproduct."[73]

Loos, though, found his supporters. Among them was a leading voice of the day, the famed German sociologist Georg Simmel. Simmel, too, called for the separation of art from objects of daily use: "The products of the arts and crafts," he wrote, "are intended to be integrated in daily life. For that reason, they represent the complete opposites of works of art, which belong to a world of their own"—a sentence that was certainly in accord with Loos's beliefs.[74]

For Loos, the whole matter finally came to a head toward the end of 1909. It was then that he received an invitation from the Berlin writer and critic Herwarth Walden to come to the German capital and give a talk. Loos had never spoken publicly before. He would later become a brilliant orator, but he was nervous, concerned that he would be unable to carry off his speech.

The event took place on November 11, 1909. Loos's title was "Kritik der angewandten Kunst" (Critique of applied art). On the day of the lecture, Loos traveled as far as Dresden, where he spent several hours preparing, before completing his journey. It is possible that he wrote out a text. It is also possible that he only made some notes. Nothing has survived.

The event took place in the gallery of the art dealer Paul Cassirer. Probably no more than thirty or forty people were in attendance. Loos had hoped the talk would stir up some controversy; he even asked Walden to make sure that the students from the Berlin Technische Hochschule were invited. But the reaction, to the extent that there was one, was tepid; a few of the local newspapers reported on the event, and they mostly summarized his comments.

When Loos repeated the talk in Vienna in early January 1910, the audience was probably larger, yet the response was still muted. Those attending already had a good sense of Loos's views, and they knew what he would say.

Loos did come up with a new title for the Vienna lecture, "Ornament and Crime," which he hoped would do just what it achieved: to fan the flames of the ornament debate. Loos evidently wrote out a full text, which he read (likely with some ad libs along the way). This appears to have been, almost verbatim, the essay that has come down to us in published form.

What has been lost to later observers is that there was little new substance in Loos's presentation. He had formulated his basic position years before. Bits and pieces of the talk appear in many of his earlier published writings. Loos did, however, change his rhetorical approach, using the idea that *producing* modern ornament was tantamount to a crime. (He never says that ornament *is* a crime). Almost everything else he recycled. Even Loos's listing of the criminals—those who still insisted on contriving new ornament, despite all else—he had used before. And unsurprisingly, Hoffmann was at the top of his roll of the accused.

The irony of all this is that by the time Loos was making his most strident attack on modern ornament, it was quickly fading. The Jugendstil was in decline, and the two dominant modes of design were a return to history (the second blush of historicism that Hoffmann was pursuing) and the newly announced fealty to "functional" forms, which would eventually morph into the *Sachlichkeit*, or objectivity, of the 1920s.

But there was yet a bigger irony. The interiors that Loos and Hoffmann were creating in those last four years before the outbreak of World War I, by the time "ornament and crime" was becoming a motto, were not so very different. Both made recourse to history, in Loos's case mostly through the use of replicas, in Hoffmann's, as we have seen, by means of an invented past; and both were promoting a specifically bourgeois aesthetic. At the time, neither had the slightest interest in designing for the working class—or even the lower middle class.

Yet by 1909, before Loos set out on his journey to Berlin, a new current was making its appearance in Viennese design. It would prove to be transformative, both in Vienna and, later, around the world.

Chapter 4

Oskar Strnad

In the firmament of young Viennese modernists in the years just before World War I, no star shone more brilliantly than Oskar Strnad (fig. 18). Almost from the moment of his first emergence, around 1909, Strnad represented a vital new direction. He was immediately recognized for his genius and, as it would turn out, all too soon forgotten.

Strnad was born in Vienna in 1879, one of seven children of Samuel Strnad and Therese (née Loury). Like many Viennese of that time, both parents had been born in the provinces, in Bohemia, and recently arrived in the capital, seeking opportunity. Samuel Strnad worked as an estate manager. At the time of Oskar's birth, the family lived on Ruprechtsplatz, across from the city's oldest church, in what was then the Jewish quarter of the inner city.[75] They moved around during his childhood, residing for a time in Györ, in western Hungary, and later in Saalfelden, in Salzburg province. After their return to Vienna, they occupied a flat in the bourgeois ninth district. The young Strnad attended a local *Realschule*, a secondary school emphasizing mathematics and the natural sciences. After graduating in 1900, he enrolled in the faculty of architecture at the Technische Hochschule. He studied there with Carl König, Karl Mayreder, Max von Ferstel, and Ferdinand Fellner—all representatives of Central European historicism at its height.[76]

Equally skilled with pencil and brush, Strnad soon became known for his graphic designs and paintings (fig. 19). The money he earned from these works, along with a travel scholarship, allowed him to undertake an extended trip in 1903, first along the Dalmatian coast and then to Rome and Ravenna. The following year, he completed his dissertation—quite exceptionally for an architecture student of that time—on early Christian architectural ornament.[77]

It was in this period that Strnad took part in the first of many architectural competitions. The exquisite drawing he submitted to a competition to design a new synagogue in Trieste offers testimony to his developing abilities (fig. 20). But he was

Fig. 18| Oskar Strnad, self-portrait, ca. 1905. Oil on board, 45.5 × 29.5 cm.

Fig. 19| Oskar Strnad, cover for Wiener Türmer magazine, 1904.

not yet ready to start his own practice, and he spent the following two years in architectural offices. Strnad first worked for the firm of Fellner & Helmer, specialists in theater design. After another trip to Italy, he joined the atelier of the neo-Baroque master Friedrich Ohmann, who was then engaged with the extension to the imperial palace. Strnad grew tired of laboring for others, and around 1906 he launched a joint practice with Oskar Wlach, one of his former classmates at the Technische Hochschule.[78] Over the next several years, they took part—unsuccessfully—in various competitions across the Habsburg lands, including the one for the new War Ministry building in Vienna. With another of his former classmates, Viktor Lurje, Strnad also submitted an entry to a competition for an elaborate arcade in the spa town of Karlsbad (Karlovy Vary).[79] It was not until 1911 that he and Wlach were able to realize their first building, an apartment house on the Stuckgasse, in Vienna's seventh district (fig. 21).[80]

Despite being wedged into a narrow and unimportant street, the structure, with its spartan, almost mute façade, was an early contribution to modernism in the

Fig. 20| Oskar Strnad, competition design for a synagoge in Triest, 1904. Motto: "Spiagge Adriatiche." Pen and ink and watercolor on paper, 36.7 × 53.8 cm.
Fig. 21| Oskar Strnad and Oskar Wlach, Hörandner apartment building, Vienna 7., Stuckgasse 14, 1910–11. Photo: Wolfgang Thaler.

city. It came at the same time as Loos's Goldman & Salatsch building on Michaelerplatz, but, despite being even more radical in its austerity, it attracted almost no attention because of its inconspicuous location. By then, Strnad had taken up an academic career teaching architecture and design at the Kunstgewerbeschule.

The appointment put Strnad in the forefront of the new generation of Viennese modernists. The visibility that came with it also meant that he began almost immediately to receive other commissions. One of those was for a villa on the city's outskirts, the Hock House (1912–13), which proved to be an important step in the development of Strnad's spatial ideas.[81] More significant for our story, however, are the interiors he was able to complete before the outbreak of the war, and what they would come to mean.

No photographs of Strnad's first interior, the Kaiser Franz Josef Marine Hospice on the Türkenstraße, completed in 1908, have survived.[82] But there are images of his next work, for his own apartment on the Ungargasse, in the third district (figs. 22, 23). They show, in nascent form, all the elements of what was to become his mature idiom.

At first glimpse, there is nothing about these spaces or furnishings that appears new or special. They give off the impression of being makeshift and unharmonious, a collection of disparate objects seemingly placed without much thought. Some of the furnishings, like the two chairs on the left in the view of the living room, look as if they belong to their time. (They closely resemble, in fact, the chairs in Hoffmann's smoking room at the 1908 Kunstschau; see figure 12.) Most of the other pieces appear to be inherited or acquired at a secondhand furniture dealer.

To an educated eye, there is a late eighteenth- or early nineteenth-century cast to the spaces. The correct historical label might be Regency (the two chairs in the foreground on the right in the living room) or perhaps Biedermeier (the oval table on the left), or a bit of each. Without examining the photographs carefully, one might be tempted to say that they are somehow Loosian. They do give the impression of having been "assembled" rather than designed. The rather informal arrangement of the pieces certainly looks nothing like the carefully tuned ensembles of Hoffmann and the other Secessionists. Few of the furnishings in Strnad's rooms match, and they are in no way architectonic, which is to say that they are placed independently of the room, its walls, floor, and ceiling. They appear to float freely, with little or no consideration given to their positioning. Strnad's reliance on older

Fig. 22| Oskar Strnad, living room in Strnad's own apartment on the Ungargasse, Vienna 3., 1909.
Fig. 23| Oskar Strnad, drop-front secretary, cabinet on stand, and chair in Strnad's apartment on the Ungargasse, Vienna 3., 1909.

forms and pieces thus seems to parallel what Loos was doing in his rooms. In truth, they are the result of a very different sensibility: they are neither as controlled nor as substantial, lighter in feel, less "settled," less bourgeois.

It is easy to dismiss these spaces as old-fashioned and fustian. Nothing about them betokens a revolution in design or points toward a novel way of living. They seem to be fixed in the orbit of late historicism and vastly less vital or forward-looking than Hoffmann's minimalism or even his later remaking of classicism.

Two aspects of Strnad's aesthetic fit precisely with the ongoing debates in Central Europe, however. The first has to do with ornament. There *is* ornament in the rooms; for example, in the Oriental rug and the seat cushions in the living space. This ornament, though, is not "new." It is not the ornament of the Jugendstil or the Secession. It is derived from older patterns—patterns that could correctly be said to be traditional. In that sense, Strnad's use of ornament is in keeping with Loos's precepts.

But the second aspect of Strnad's apartment deviates from Loos's design principles. Loos tended to use older furnishings in the form of replicas—precise copies of the originals. He was particularly fond of Hepplewhite or Chippendale chairs, which he thought of as consummate examples of past design. In his mind, they required no alteration or adjustment. It is difficult to tell from the grainy photographs, but it appears that only some of the furnishings Strnad employed fall into this category. Others look not be replicas but antiques—originals. This seems to be the case with the Biedermeier oval table in the living room and possibly the chest of drawers behind it. And the pieces that are not originals are not replicas; they are instead creative reworkings of older styles. This is true for the drop-front desk and the cabinet on stand in the corner space. Although they borrow from older stylistic ideas, they represent a reinvented past.

By that definition, they could be described as exemplars of late historicism. Here, though, the differences between what Strnad and others at the time were doing are small but telling. Late Viennese historicism was closely bound up with the various classically derived form-languages—the neo-Baroque or the neo-Rococo, for instance. To the extent that these styles were reclaimed, it was often in a way intended to make them more elaborated. This was precisely Hoffmann's tactic. It would lead him (and the young Dagobert Peche) in subsequent years to a modern "ultra-Rococo."

The other neoclassical revival available to the Viennese, the Biedermeier revival, had begun a few years before and presented different opportunities. Because the furnishings were already quite pared down, they required little adjustment. Most designers undertook minor redesigns, and many simply installed originals in their spaces. By 1909, Strnad was already moving away from both direct appropriation and greater elaboration. He would never abandon either one entirely, but he began instead to mine other sources: the European vernacular and—though it is not yet evident here—Western archaism.

Strnad's interest in the vernacular is notably present in two of the chairs in these photos: the small chair positioned between the drop-front desk and the cabinet on stand in the corner space, and the ladderback chair on the left side of the living room facing the chest of drawers. Both chairs are based on earlier English pieces. In their immediate origins, these are folk designs, the furniture not of the elites but of ordinary people. The smaller chair is a classic "turner's chair," or "thrown" or "spindle" chair, made up of individual spindles carved on a lathe. Such chairs were popular in the sixteenth and seventeenth centuries in England, as well in New England and the Netherlands. Strnad's version, however, is in the form of a Windsor chair, most common in the eighteenth century. His version is not a replica. Rather, it is a "designed" piece; it is truncated and simplified, and in that way made inherently more modern.

The other piece, the ladderback chair in the living room, is the product of a similar form of appropriation but more radical in its alterations. Strnad made a number of these chairs; they figure in his interiors at least until the war (fig. 24). They are based on English models dating to the time of George III. Strnad's more immediate source, however, was likely not the original version of this design but a reimagining of the same form made by Ernest Gimson in the late nineteenth century.

Gimson, whom Nikolaus Pevsner once called "the greatest of the English architect-designers," was aligned with the Arts and Crafts movement. He was deeply involved in the effort to reapply past forms in a manner that suited modern life, and, consequently, his work was an important source for some of the Viennese modernists.[83]

One of Gimson's ladderback chairs in the Victoria & Albert Museum reflects the exquisite craftmanship associated with his furniture. But it is also a sophisticated effort at refinement (fig. 25), the product of a considered process of adaptation and reduction. Strnad's chair, if less elemental, is more dramatic than Gimson's version. He, too, smoothed and pared down the legs and arms, but he exaggerated the finials and the crossrails of the back. The result is not exactly verisimilitude; rather, it is something more like an homage, an updated remembrance of a former time. Strnad seems to be suggesting both that the past can be mined for intrinsically modern objects and ideas, and that the past can be creatively refashioned to fit the present.

He is also stating something more consequential for the future of Viennese modernism: that in the process of finding the way to a modern expression, the past does not need to be cast off. The present—which is always advancing—also inevitably includes the past, whether immediate or distant. There is no reason to reject it: to do so is to lie about the reality of culture; namely, that it is continuous. This is precisely the argument Loos had made.

Strnad's idea of continuity undoubtedly owed much to Loos's thinking. During his student years, he and several of his classmates at the Technische Hochschule often sat at Loos's table at the nearby Café Museum, listening to the older man hold forth on his views about modernism. Strnad, though, was never a true follower of

Fig. 24| Oskar Strnad, ladderback armchair, designed ca. 1909; this example ca. 1912. Beechwood with braided straw seat, 105 × 63.5 × 47 cm.

Fig. 25| Ernest Gimson, ladderback armchair, made ca. 1892–1904.

Loos. He saw in Loos's cultural thinking a way of understanding and responding to the needs of modern life, and echoes of Loos's thinking show up in his work ever after. But he preferred to pursue his own path, both formally and intellectually.

Strnad also took important lessons from Hoffmann. In particular, he shared Hoffmann's abiding faith in the classical tradition and its potential as a source for a new design language. We see hints of this in a color depiction Strand produced in 1907 of the Parthenon as it might have appeared in its heyday (fig. 26). It was a decidedly sanitized version of the temple—the sort of objectification of the classical that was also becoming increasingly important for Hoffmann in those years.

We can also witness the two men's close relationship in the decorations Strnad made for Hoffmann's pavilion at the 1911 International Art Exhibition in Rome. Hoffmann was responsible for the overall design, a U-shaped temple to art that borrowed broadly from Hellenistic precedents and—almost certainly in detail—from the recently excavated Altar of Zeus in Pergamon. Hoffmann's version was more delicate than the Pergamon altar, inscribed with an almost Biedermeier-like sensibility. (His other inspiration may have been the *Salettl*, the garden pavilions or follies popular in Vienna in the late eighteenth and early nineteenth centuries.) The building housed a collection of Klimt paintings; the sculptures placed throughout were the work of Anton Hanak and Franz Barwig.

Strnad's contribution was minor by comparison: small painted plaster reliefs that were applied to the wall surfaces of the pavilion inside and out. One is visible in a photograph of the building taken at an oblique angle from the left front side (fig. 27). But this little relief resembles less the sculpture program of the Pergamon altar (an enormous frieze depicting the battle of the giants and the gods, writhing in their exertions and suffering visibly) than the almost naïve portrayals of the preclassical age. In form and feeling, they are closer to the representations of an archaic art.

Strnad was not alone in turning to the earliest sources of Western art, to ancient Egypt and the Mycenean and Minoan cultures. The notion that the preclassical could provide a basis for a new art was also shared by many of the Secessionists. The reasons were several, as Anthony Alofsin succinctly laid out some years ago: "first they were interested in the repudiation of nineteenth-century historicism and the search for a 'real history' found in basic pure forms. Secondly, they wanted to go back to *Ur*-forms and understand the primal meanings those forms represented. Thirdly, the Secessionists wanted to connect their own designs to those pure beginnings of culture itself. Finally, they were drawn not only to the symbolism of antiquity and exotic cultures but also to the abstract, bold graphic qualities found in artifacts in those cultures."[84]

Strnad subscribed to all these ambitions. Even before the Rome exhibition opened, he and Lurje installed a "garden room," based on preclassical Minoan and Mycenean decorations, at the Second Exhibition of Austrian Applied Art held at the

Fig. 26| Oskar Strnad, *Der Parthenon*, 1907. Lithographic print, K.k. Hof- und Staatsdruckerei, Vienna.
Fig. 27| Josef Hoffmann, Austrian Pavilion at the International Art Exhibition, Rome, 1911.

Austrian Museum for Art and Industry (the institution that would later become the Museum für angewandte Kunst, MAK), which ran from late October 1910 to early February 1911.

The oddly disjointed space—which also featured a Secessionist-inspired settee and chairs designed by Josef Zotti and made by Prag-Rudniker Korbwaren—had at its center a fountain surmounted by a male figure in clay; surrounding it were painted columns and a decorated ceiling. Minus the Zotti pieces, which in no way belonged to the scene, the whole looked like a kitschy film set of a Mycenean megaron (fig. 28).[85] But Strnad and Lurje did have a serious message: that such forms constituted the beginnings of the Western tradition and that returning to them or, at least, reviving their essential simplicity could offer a viable path to artistic renewal.

Very quickly, Strnad and Lurje moved to a more sophisticated expression, less slapdash in its execution and more refined in its form-language. They unveiled it at the next exhibition at the Austrian Museum for Art and Industry, which took place in the winter months of 1911 and 1912. The full installation, which included various case pieces, a lighting fixture, and decorative and architectonic elements, was a joint project of Strnad, Lurje, and two of their fellow students at the Technische Hochschule, Josef Frank and Hugo Gorge (figs. 29–31).[86] The space also included embroidered pieces made by Strnad's wife, Mathilde (née Zipper), and Lurje's sister Mela (Melanie).[86] Some of the individual designs displayed the bold graphic patterning that was characteristic of Viennese modernism, and there were examples of the studied reductivism of the previous years (such as the small side tables at the center of figs. 29 and 31). Spread throughout, though, were hints of the simple archaic forms that Strnad had shown before. Much more than in the 1910–11 installation, these forms have been recast. The pieces seem to hark back to a distant past (or, in some instances, to Renaissance models). They are not replicas; they are designed objects.

The underlying strategy for all these designers was essentially the same: they took the basic forms of each object from a historical model, while modifying their surfaces. In most of the pieces, this involved new types of ornamentation, always with a surface patterning or language that was not in the originals.

Two years before, Strnad had investigated this idea in a pair of grave markers. One, for a couple named Thenen, he developed as an extended triangle; the other, for his own family, was a modest triangular pediment (figs. 32, 33). To these, he added "modern" inscriptions. What both have in common, aside from their nods to protoclassicism, is that they are architectonic—almost as if they were isolated parts of a building.

The full expression of this latter idea—employing such decorative elements constructively or to make space—became the next tactic Strnad examined. He did so in another "garden room," this time at the 1912 Spring Exhibition at the Museum for Art and Industry. The general look of the space was that of a Roman building, perhaps a second-century basilica, but one adapted to a domestic

Fig. 28| Oskar Strnad and Viktor Lurje, garden room (Interior I) at the Second Exhibition of Austrian Applied Art at the Austrian Museum for Art and Industry, Vienna, 1910–11.

Fig. 29| Oskar Strnad, Josef Frank, Hugo Gorge, and Viktor Lurje, Room 2 at the Winter Exhibition at the Austrian Museum for Art and Industry, Vienna, 1911–12.

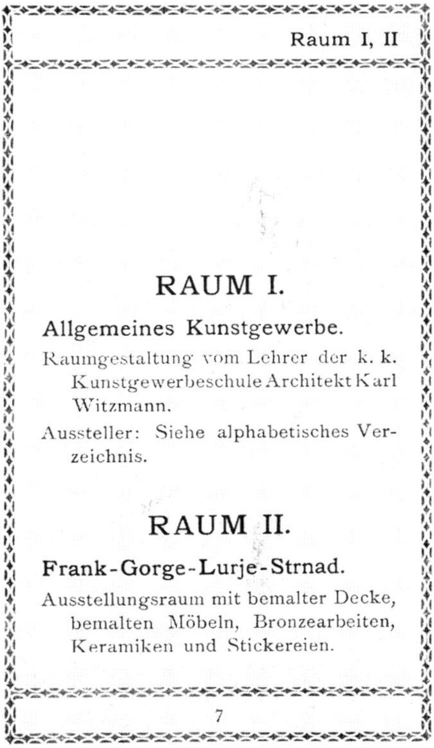

Raum I, II

RAUM I.

Allgemeines Kunstgewerbe.

Raumgestaltung vom Lehrer der k. k. Kunstgewerbeschule Architekt Karl Witzmann.

Aussteller: Siehe alphabetisches Verzeichnis.

RAUM II.

Frank-Gorge-Lurje-Strnad.

Ausstellungsraum mit bemalter Decke, bemalten Möbeln, Bronzearbeiten, Keramiken und Stickereien.

7

Fig. 30| Catalogue page listing Strnad and Lurje's contribution to the Winter Exhibition at the Austrian Museum for Art and Industry, Vienna, 1911–12. *Ausstellung Österreichischer Kunstgewerbe* 1911–1912, exh. cat.

Fig. 31| Josef Frank, Hugo Gorge, Viktor Lurje, Oskar Strnad, and Oskar Wlach, Room 2 at the Winter Exhibition at the Austrian Museum for Art and Industry, Vienna, 1911–12.
Fig. 32| Oskar Strnad, grave marker for the Thenen family, 1909.
Fig. 33| Oskar Strnad, grave marker for Samuel Jakob and Martha Strnad, 1908.

HIRSCH·THENEN
GEBOREN·11·FEBER·1831
IN·TYSMIENITZ
IN·GALIZIEN
AM·ABEND·DES
24·APRIL·1909
IN·WIEN
GESTOR
BEN
REBEKKA·THENEN
GEBOREN·21·AUGUST·1834
IN·TYSMIENITZ
IN·GALIZIEN
AM·ABEND·DES
21·APRIL·1909
IN·WIEN
GESTOR
BEN

SAMUEL
STRNAD

Fig. 34| Oskar Strnad, garden room (Room XVI) at the 1912 Spring Exhibition at the Austrian Museum for Art and Industry, Vienna. Furniture executed by Carl Bamberger; brickwork, floors, and walls by Brüder Schwadron.
Fig. 35| Oskar Strnad, garden room (Room XVI) at the 1912 Spring Exhibition at the Austrian Museum for Art and Industry, Vienna. Photo: Bruno Reiffenstein.

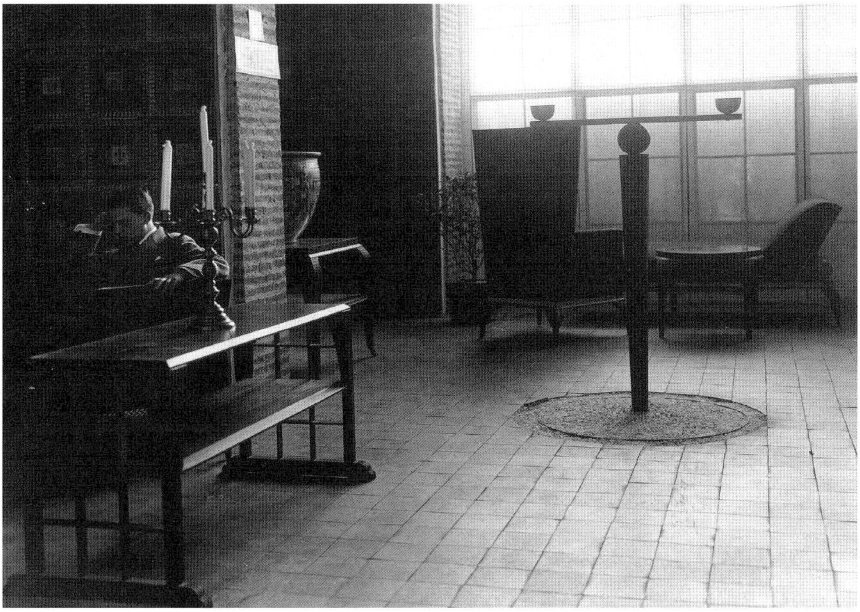

arrangement (fig. 34). In addition to a fireplace area set up in the form of an inglenook, there were also several seating ensembles and, somewhat incongruously in the middle of the room, a freestanding parrot perch (fig. 35).

The space is replete with references to Roman or earlier classical features: the Roman brick, the arches, and the applied coffering. There are also pure forms, in the parrot perch, for example, with its orb and two hemispherical bowls. Strnad, who can be seen in one of the photographs, sitting in the "inglenook" in considered contemplation, seems to be making a statement about living in the present (fig. 36). Not only is the design of the space bound up with the past (or a continuous present), but he is also saying that it might provide a guide for a new way of being in a domestic setting. It is open, relaxed, and unencumbered by formulas; the furnishings appear to be placed freely in the room, almost indiscriminately. There is no requirement to follow specific aesthetic strictures, to match the furnishings, or to forge a harmonious decorative program. Everything ostensibly goes together.

All this taken together is a critique, if a subtle one. Strnad's target was the *Gesamtkunstwerk* ideal of the Secessionists—the notion that everything in a room, every object, every piece of furniture, every textile or wall covering—should speak the same language of form and pattern, that it should all fit together precisely as one visual whole. What he is stating instead is that one should live without such rules, freely.

Fig. 36| Oskar Strnad, garden room (Room XVI) at the 1912 Spring Exhibition at the Austrian Museum for Art and Industry, Vienna. Photo: Bruno Reiffenstein.

The 1912 Spring Exhibition proved to be a landmark moment in the history of modernism. Not only was it intended to offer a summary of Austrian arts and crafts production, but it was also timed to coincide with the fifth annual meeting of the German Werkbund, in Vienna that June.[80] Carl Witzmann, a former student of Hoffmann's and a professor at the Kunstgewerbeschule (alongside Hoffmann and Strnad), curated the show. The expectation on the part of the Austrians, who formed their own branch of the Werkbund, the Österreichischer Werkbund, that summer, was that they would show their German guests a unified aesthetic conception.[89]

Instead, at least four distinct varieties of modernism were on view. One was a holdover: the swirling, vegetal look of the early Jugendstil, which was still popular then, especially in the schools and with commercial producers. The second was the language of purism and abstract geometry, which Hoffmann and most of his followers had already mostly or entirely abandoned but which yet held some currency. The third was the language of a modernized classicism, either in its original Greco-Roman guise or filtered through the later revivals, the Renaissance, the Baroque, the Rococo, and the Biedermeier—or some combination of them. This was the direction that Hoffmann was now pursuing. The fourth was the new look put forward by Strnad and the others in his circle, which now included Frank, Gorge, Lurje, and Wlach. There could have conceivably been a fifth, the idiosyncratic domestic ideal of Loos, but he remained completely outside the mainstream, the Austrian Museum, and the Werkbund.

The revolutionary cast of the presentations by Strnad and those in his circle becomes evident in comparison with the others. The first direction can be seen in the entrance to the Kunstgewerbeschule displays, which was fronted by a wall painting by Wilhelm Friedrich, a student at the school (fig. 37). It was an essay in sinuous decoration and inchoate forms. The second was represented by Robert Örley, then the president of the Secession. His remarkable "garden room" featured precast-concrete wall panels and a seating ensemble made of particle board. It was highly advanced in terms of its materials, but it belonged stylistically to the Viennese modernism of a few years before (fig. 38). Hoffmann's dining room, with its fluted walls, Rococo- and Biedermeier-inspired table, chairs, and sideboard, was the last word in chic in 1912, an updated *Gesamtkunstwerk* in the language of a modernized classicism (fig. 39). And then there was the young Josef Frank's living room (fig. 40). Frank had recently completed his studies at the Technische Hochschule. It was he and Strnad who, together with Wlach and Gorge, would promote the new direction in Viennese design, the reaction against the Secession and the Jugendstil. His living hall borrowed from the English Arts and Crafts ethos, but it also proffered something novel, a strong sense of informality and relaxation.

Hoffmann and his followers dominated the 1912 Spring Exhibition. And over the next two years they would also receive much of the publicity in the leading design journals. Strnad and his close associates, however, were working quietly to overturn all that they espoused.

Fig. 37| Wilhelm Friedrich, wall painting framing the entrance to Room XX at the 1912 Spring Exhibition at the Austrian Museum for Art and Industry, featuring the displays of the Vienna School of Arts and Crafts.

Their response came in sundry ways. In those last years before the outbreak of the war, Strnad designed and built a large villa on the city's western edge, the Wassermann House. By this time, he had formed a working partnership with Wlach and Frank. They listed themselves in publications as Strnad-Wlach-Frank, with offices in Strnad's suite of rooms in the Kunstgewerbeschule.

Strnad also created several extensive and elaborate interiors for wealthy clients in this period. One, completed in 1912, was for a family named Waller. More important, however, were two grand apartments for clients in the Gründerzeit Quarter just behind the parliament, city hall, and university.

Fig. 38| Robert Örley, garden room (Room XV) at the 1912 Spring Exhibition at the Austrian Museum for Art and Industry. Chairs and tables executed by Pressstoff-Möbel-Gesellschaft M.B.H., Vienna.
Fig. 39| Josef Hoffmann, dining room (Room IX) at the 1912 Spring Exhibition at the Austrian Museum for Art and Industry, executed by J. Soulek, Vienna.
Fig. 40| Josef Frank, living room (Room XIII) at the 1912 Spring Exhibition at the Austrian Museum for Art and Industry.

The apartment for factory owner Fritz Hirsch, at Reichsratsstraße 1, was the finest and most ostentatious of Strnad's prewar interiors. It was in the best sense *großbürgerlich*, a direct expression of haute bourgeois taste and aspirations. Strnad lavished on his wealthy client the most exquisite finishes and materials. The living room, with its coffered and painted ceiling, unique furnishings, and splendid textiles, perfectly expressed the will to opulence of that class and time (figs. 41, 42). Everything was custom made, testimony to the skill of Vienna's consummate artisans.

Here and there, though, are glimpses of a modernity that might have been found in the interiors of the Secessionists or Loos. The light fixture in the large dining room—unencumbered and immediate in its formal expression—speaks of a newness that seems at odds with the formality and luxury of the rest of the room (fig. 43). Yet even where Strnad appears to be most traditional—in the immensely long sideboard that extended almost the full length of the back wall—he is pursuing an unconventional agenda (fig. 44). The piece *looks* antique; its motifs and arrangement hark back to eighteenth-century models. But the effect is more like that of a subversive historicism, as if, by means of studied exaggeration and manipulation, Strnad was contriving something other. Even the crib in the *Kinderzimmer*, the children's room, plays with tradition, for it is at once part garden arbor, part modern whimsy (fig. 45).

Yet to see only the splendor or the novelty of these rooms is to miss what is most important. What Strnad is aiming for—aside from pleasing a client with deep pockets—is livability. Far more than Hoffmann and the other Secessionists, he wanted to give his inhabitants comfort. And here, he understood that in both senses: physical and psychological. The individual seating pieces are cushioned, and the areas one touches, the arms and backs, are softened and smoothed. Every surface throughout the apartment (except in the service spaces) is fashioned in such a manner that its haptic qualities are considered. It is all "pleasant to the touch," even the door handles, which Strnad took care to design himself.

Strnad was also concerned with the mental impressions he created. The spaces are about accommodation, allowing the inhabitants to move about readily. The paths from place to place are natural; there are neither long axial passageways nor any fixed formality. Most of the seating pieces and tables can be moved or shifted to adapt to quite varied activities.

The contrast here with Hoffmann's rooms is sharp. Hoffmann intended his "assemblies" to remain in place; they were fixed mise-en-scènes. The "professor" had made them thus, and they were not to be altered, lest the harmony of the space be lost.

Loos had made light of precisely this aspect of Hoffmann's designs in his 1900 essay "Vom armen reichen Mann" (The poor rich man). He writes of the client who mistakenly despoiled his expensive architect-designed living room by wearing slippers created for the bedroom.[90] But Loos's own interiors also had about them a sense of "completeness." Loos's furnishings were often large, heavy, and not readily moved.

Fig. 41| Oskar Strnad, salon, Fritz Hirsch Apartment, Vienna 1., Reichsratsstraße 1, 1913.
Fig. 42| Oskar Strnad, commode, Hirsch Apartment.

Fig. 43| Oskar Strnad, dining room, Hirsch Apartment.
Fig. 44| Oskar Strnad, sideboard, Hirsch Apartment.

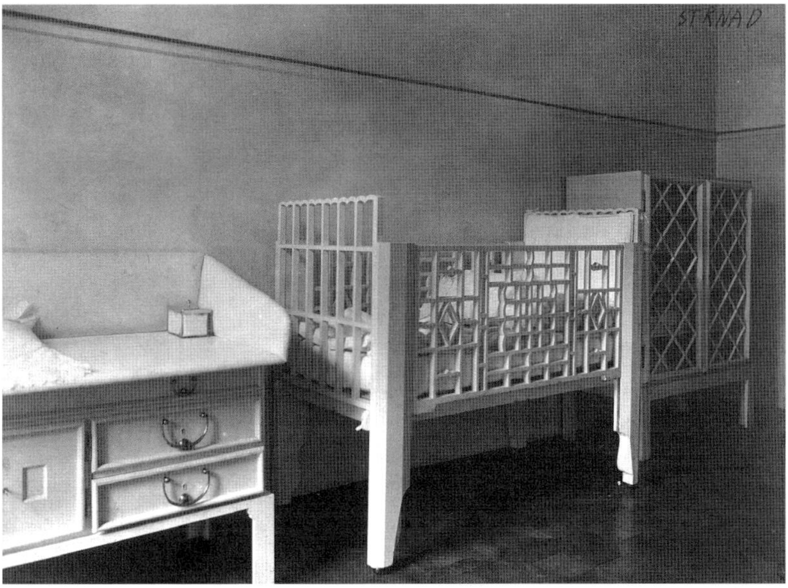

Fig. 45| Oskar Strnad, children's room, Hirsch Apartment.
Fig. 46| Oskar Strnad, living room in the Wilhelm Hellmann Apartment, Vienna 1., Rathausstraße 17, Vienna, 1914.

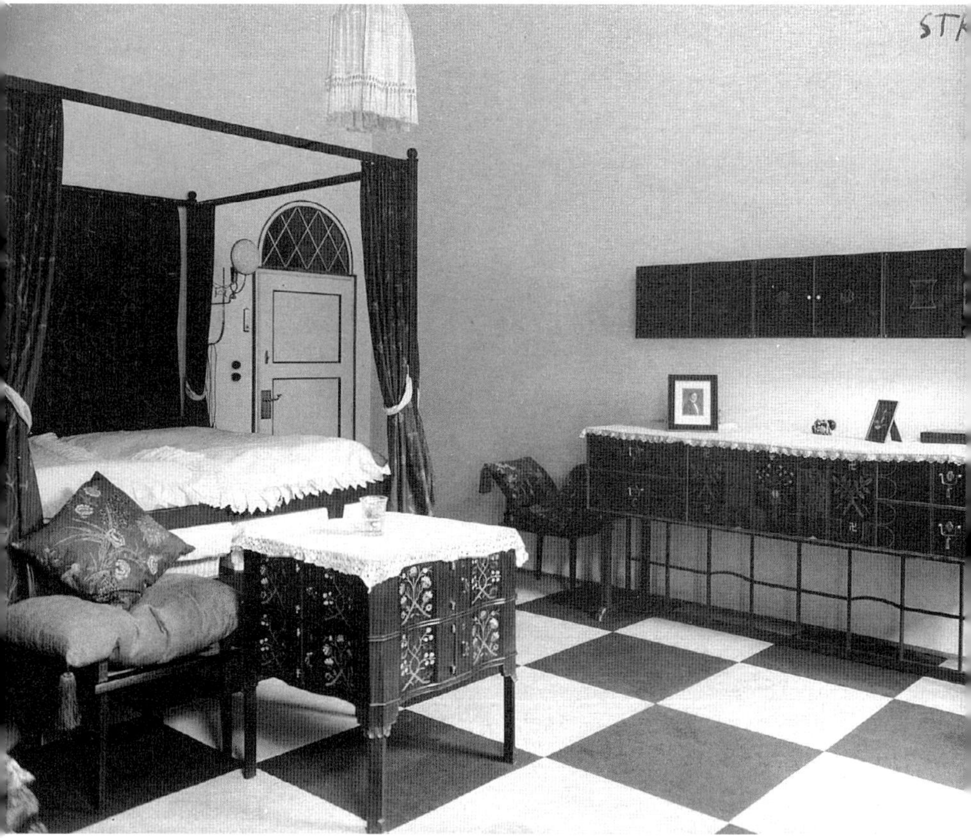

Fig. 47| Oskar Strnad, bedroom, Hellmann Apartment.
Fig. 48| Oskar Strnad, secretary, Hellmann Apartment.

STRNAD

Fig. 49| Oskar Strnad, armchair, Hellmann Apartment.

They may not have "matched," but they appeared nonetheless "set." In Strnad's Hirsch interiors, the difference from Loos's approach is not large. There is still something cumbrous about it all, but he was heading in a quite different direction.

There are hints of this new course in the second grand apartment Strnad completed in 1914, for another wealthy industrialist, Wilhelm Hellmann. The apartment, at Rathausstraße 17, just across from the Votivkirche, shared many features of the Hirsch rooms: the same luxury of materials and the unmistakable air of nouveau riche taste (fig. 46). Here, though, the rooms are more intimate and considerably smaller. The living room has an almost Biedermeier feel, especially the cozy corner sitting area. The principal bedroom, by contrast, is more open, airier, and, in its relative modesty, more obviously modern (fig. 47).

Throughout the apartment were examples of Strnad's characteristic amalgam of old forms and new decoration. A small secretary he designed offers hints of Expressionism and the jutting and angular forms of contemporary Czech Cubism—all set into what seems to be an understated Rococo frame (fig. 48). The apartment also had one of Strnad's most eccentric chairs, an exuberant merging of Windsor and "turner" styles (fig. 49).

As with so much else he was making in these years, it would be easy to dismiss this object as a trice of historical fantasy or the final breath of the old historicism. In a sense, it was both. But like everything Strnad was doing in these spaces, it was also something else. It was a novel way of thinking about the interior, the beginning of an idea of how we should live.

Chapter 5

Wiener Wohnkultur

In the early spring of 1914, Strnad presented a short lecture series on home decoration at the Vienna Urania, an adult education center at the edge of the inner city. He gave three lectures in all, on successive Tuesdays. The first had to do with the arrangement of living spaces, the second with the placement of furnishings, and the third with decorating with accessories.[91]

Strnad spoke from prepared texts—the typescript pages still exist—though he probably improvised at times. Each lecture must have lasted about forty-five minutes. The whole presentation was scheduled to run for an hour, with a promised question-and-answer period at the end. The typescript reveals that Strnad sometimes fell into Viennese dialect, and there are hints here and there of the Bohemian-inflected German his parents spoke.[92]

Strnad certainly did not intend these talks—which were geared for young brides—to present a theoretical statement.[93] Yet they do offer insight into his emerging ideas, especially about the meanings of modernity. One of his most compelling statements comes at the start of the first lecture. It has to do with style, and why style in his view was not the true mark of modernism:

> When a man goes to the tailor and orders a tailcoat, he is doing so to look elegant. But he doesn't order a decorated tailcoat. He doesn't order a tailcoat

> of a certain style; he simply orders a tailcoat. Everyone knows what a tailcoat should look like. At most, there are differences in the quality of the fabric or in the choice of the tailor. I want to tell you a story: "An Englishwoman was invited to a country gentry dinner party and was asked afterward how she enjoyed it. 'I've never seen so many bad tails at once,' she answered." We judge the quality of tailcoats by the way they fit, how they are worn. How easily does one distinguish a good tailcoat from a bad one, or, if you like, an ugly tailcoat from a beautiful one! But if I were to ask you how you do so, you will hardly be able to say precisely, but it would not have to do with style.[94]

Strnad's point is that elegance and correctness define beauty in such dress clothes. The tendency of his time was to think about interiors not in this way but, rather, as momentary fashion. This practice was at odds with the real function of interiors, he insisted, since they had to last—and look appropriate for a much longer time. This is a point that Loos, too, had made repeatedly. Strnad also notes, like Loos, that objects of daily use are "good and fitting" only when they are practical or functional. Strnad did not reject the notion of style—any more than Loos had—he merely thought that style alone should not drive the design of interiors. Greatly more important for him were the impressions one gained from being in a particular space—whether that space was *gemütlich*, homey and agreeable, and whether it allowed the inhabitants' lives to unfold freely.

Strnad offered a related argument about ornament in the lectures. It follows Loos's assertions that ornament was not only fading away but wasteful and inappropriate in modern times. Strnad writes that a string of pearls or a single diamond might be suitable for a woman to wear on the right occasion, and that apartments in the same way might display some form of enrichment if the dominant theme was reserve and plainness.[95] He also specifically takes on the question of industrially produced ornament, condemning it *unmoralisch* (amoral) because it violated his conviction that ornament was personal and thus should only be made by hand.

In the Urania lectures, it becomes clear that Strnad shared Loos's notion that the modern interior should be an assemblage, pieced together from sundry sources. He viewed decorating in great part as "selecting"—searching in the marketplace for what suited a given person's needs and the times. A great part of each of his three lectures is taken up with how to source furnishings and decorative objects—specifically how one should decide what was appropriate for modern times and where one might find the best pieces.

Yet Strnad drew quite different conclusions about what such assembling meant. He laid these out—as prescriptions or suggestions—in an article he published just after the war.

"Neue Wege in der Wohnungs-Einrichtung" (New ways to furnish living spaces) is a capsule of Strnad's design strategies.[96] (It is reproduced in the appendix, in translation.) It is also a description of the new direction in Viennese design he helped to foster, a constellation of thoughts about aesthetics and living that would become known as the *Wiener Wohnkultur*—literally, the Viennese living culture.

Strnad is precise about its features. Paint the walls white, for example, he tells his readers. Never use wallpaper; it is too busy and tends to dematerialize the wall. Ensure that the edges of a room—the places where the floor meets the wall and where the wall meets the ceiling—are visible. Don't place objects or furnishings in the corners. Don't use wall-to-wall-carpets, but rather several small rugs. Decorate the walls with handcrafted fabrics. Don't hang prints. Use only original art. Underfurnish. Always prefer informality and openness to "completeness" or forced symmetries. And so on.[97] Taken together, these basic principles yielded a markedly different conception of living spaces, a break from everything the Viennese modernists had been doing up to this moment.

Strnad was not the sole author of this shift—a shift away, it should be said again, from both the Hoffmannesque and the Loosian. He was aided, and later superseded, by his former classmates from the Technische Hochschule: Lurje, Wlach, Gorge, Walter Sobotka (who was younger and entered the school after Strnad had graduated), and, most importantly, Frank.[98]

At first, the new look they were constructing appeared to be merely another form of historicism, updated but not in any sense "other." That was true of their jointly designed space for the 1911–12 Winter Exhibition. And it was mostly true for Strnad's two bourgeois apartments in the Rathaus quarter. But already at the 1912 Spring Exhibition there were clear signs of a novel direction, most visible on the window side of the room Frank installed. (fig. 50; cf. fig. 40). It was exactly as Strnad described: light, airy, and with minimal furnishings. Those furnishings—three ladderback chairs, a dropleaf table, a settee, and sideboard—were themselves thinned (i.e., more attenuated than the originals) and unencumbered. The only ornament in the space was the checkerboard patterning of the floor, and the cushions, which were covered with handloomed textiles.

There are distinct historical references in this space. The checkerboard floor is doubtless an homage to the Dutch seventeenth century (perhaps the "architectonic" paintings of Vermeer); the table, chairs, and settee borrow from English and Austrian eighteenth-century precedents; the sideboard draws closely from the designs of Gimson and Sidney and Ernest Barnsley—some of the best crafters of the English Arts and Crafts movement. But it is not a historicist collage. Instead, it is a statement about restraint, purity, and unfettered living. The references to the past are secondary.

Still, these references have a function: they are meant to speak about continuity, about an attachment to the past. Strnad and the others, as we have seen, rejected the idea that modernism represented a complete break, that only by rejecting the past could one find one's way to a new aesthetic. The historical forms for them operate as reminders of this connection (in that sense, they are related to nostalgia),

Fig. 50| Josef Frank, living room (Room XIII) at the 1912 Spring Exhibition at the Austrian Museum for Art and Industry.
Fig. 51| Oskar Strnad, living room in an apartment in Vienna 19., 1912.
Fig. 52| Oskar Strnad, office in an apartment in Vienna 19., 1912.

but they also are aides-mémoires of quality and propriety. They saw the great design of the past as something that could be retained precisely because it embodied these features.

Strnad contributed most conspicuously to the rise of the new Wohnkultur in another way: promoting the ideas of comfort and leisure in his spaces. The living room and office he designed for an unknown client in Vienna's nineteenth district in 1912 are discourses on "pleasantness"—making place for everyday life to unfold, amiably, and free of any stylistic or theoretical demands (figs. 51, 52). The critic Max Eisler would later observe that Strnad and the others intended such softened seating pieces and unfussy appointments to offer a sense of refuge from the demands of everyday life and the workplace.[99] But Strnad was also seeking two other effects: the sense of domesticity he saw in contemporary British interiors, and what one might call "ordinariness."

In rejecting the search for style as the primary focus of modern interiors, he was also calling into question the idea of design itself. The two 1912 apartment rooms betray no direct evidence of the designer's hand: they could readily be the result of a casual process of buying and arranging on the part of the occupants. There is an underlying scheme—modern yet understated—but it is by no means obvious.

Strnad's most complete interior of the years before the war, which he designed for the Wassermann House with the assistance of Wlach, operates in a similar way, though it is more unassuming. The clients were Jakob Wassermann, a well-known German writer of the day, and his wife—and fellow writer—Julie (née Speyer); the site was then a mostly unbuilt area along the western edge of the city.

The house is basically in the form of an L, with the main living areas in the rear (fig. 53). Strnad employed a palate of furnishings like those in the 1912 apartment, but far fewer of them. The result was a sense of opening, flowing space, with "islands" of furniture placed here and there (figs. 54, 55). The white walls and the relative paucity of art or decorative pieces only enhanced that look. On the one hand, the sensibility was almost that of a highly reduced Biedermeier; but it all appeared surprisingly modern, despite the quasi-historicist touches.

This seeming informality betrayed the fact that it was all very carefully set out. Strnad and Wlach (who evidently saw to the details and execution of the individual objects) considered every selection and planned the placement of every piece. Strnad prepared elevations of the principal spaces (fig. 56). These drawings, more than any other document, reveal the truth about Strnad's aesthetic. In photographs, the spaces appear sunny and carefree. In rendered form, one sees how considered the whole interior was.

Otto Niedermoser, who studied with Strnad in the late 1910s and early 1920s and later became his assistant, understood, perhaps better than anyone, what Strnad was doing: "Strnad was never provocative," he wrote. "[H]e was determined and sought always to present his ideas in such a fashion that they were natural and unobtrusive, so that for the casual observer hardly anything would stand out. In

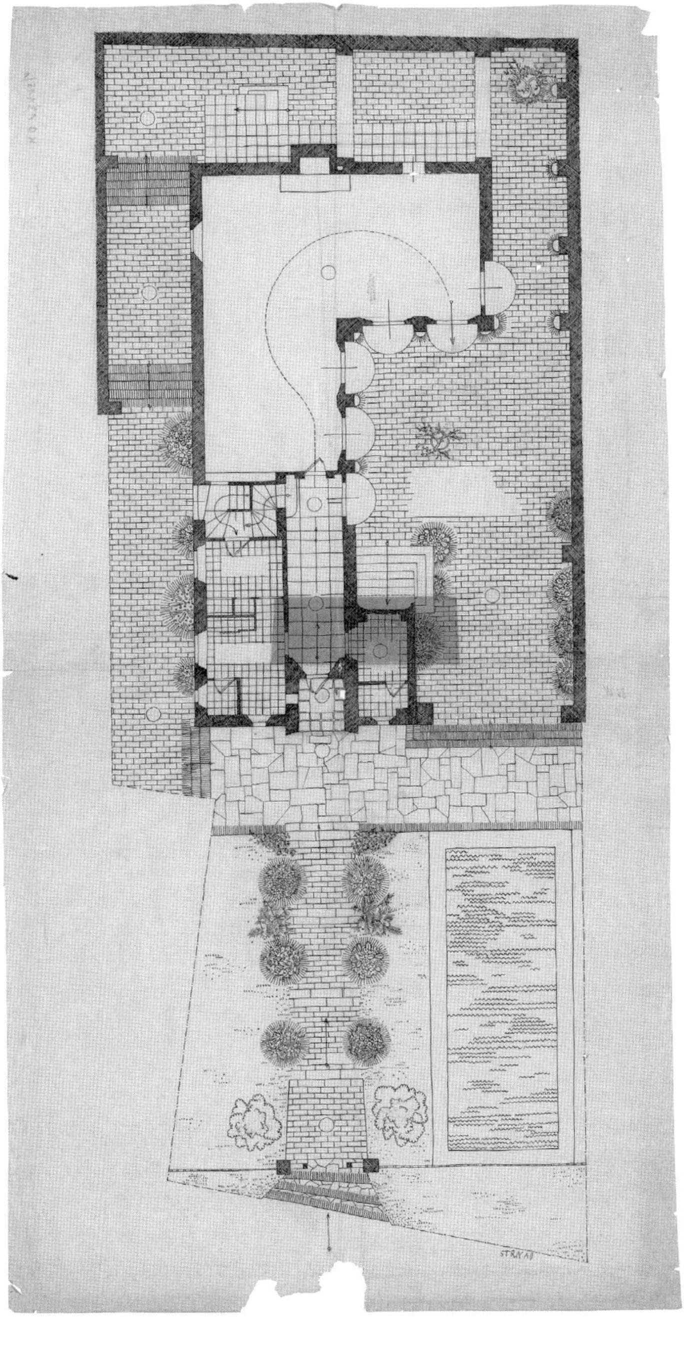

Fig. 53| Oskar Strnad with Oskar Wlach, ground-floor plan of the Wassermann House, Vienna 19., Paul-Ehrlich-Gasse 4, 1912–15.

Fig. 54| Oskar Strnad with Oskar Wlach, living room, view toward the music space, Wassermann House, 1912–15.
Fig. 55| Oskar Strnad with Oskar Wlach, living room, Wassermann House.

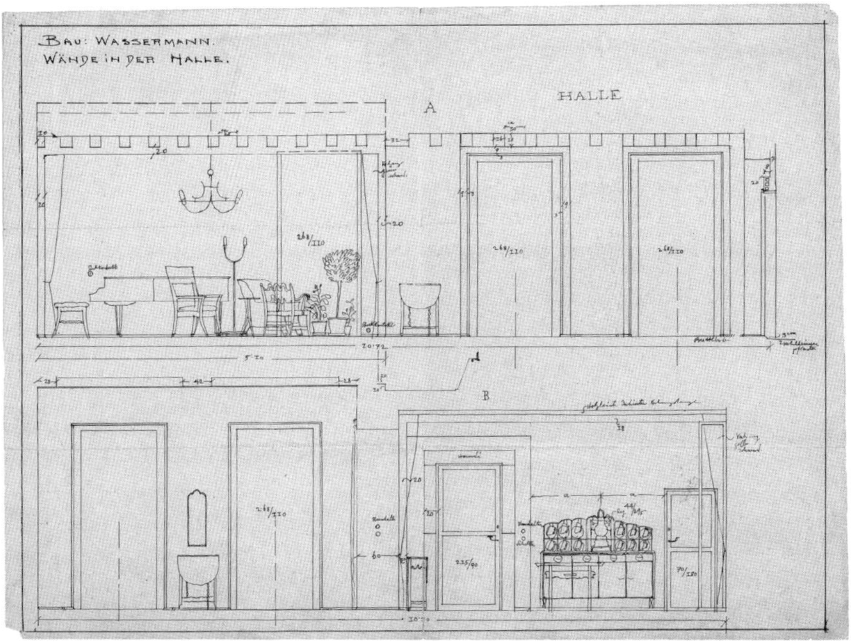

Fig. 56| Oskar Strnad, elevation of the wall in the Wassermann House, 1914.
Fig. 57| Oskar Strnad (Strnad, Wlach, Frank), office, ca. 1914.

contradistinction to the other modern artists of his time, who for a time dressed the old conventions in new forms, [Strnad] created (for a time with conventional forms) new content."[100] Put differently, Strnad was speaking about modern life, but doing so with the old vocabulary. He was—and Niedermoser gets this right—"a silent revolutionary."[101]

For the younger members of the Strnad circle, this wasn't enough. What Frank and Gorge brought to the new Wohnkultur was far greater reticence and less discernible borrowings from the past.

A first indication of this is in another of Strnad's designs, for an office space for an unknown client around 1914 (fig. 57). The two chairs and the table were typical for him—new but appearing to be old. The large case pieces, however, were manifestly different. They are well conceived and surprisingly modern. Both borrow from English Arts and Crafts ideals, albeit indirectly. The larger of the two, set against the back wall, could almost come from the 1950s or 1960s. It is splendidly reduced and modular. Yet in comparison with what came next, Strnad's approach was still cautious.

Frank, by 1912, although six years younger than Strnad, was already becoming the other leading light of this new design movement (fig. 58). Born in Vienna, he, like Strnad, Lurje, Gorge, and Wlach, was the son of an assimilated Jewish middle-class family.[102] Frank's father was a textile merchant, and he grew up in the inner city, coincidently in the same building where the writer Hermann Broch's family lived.[103] Frank had entered the architecture department at the Technische Hochschule a year before Strnad completed his dissertation. He, too, wrote a dissertation—his was on the original appearances of the churches of Leon Battista Alberti—and he graduated in 1910 with a doctorate in architecture.[104]

Frank's first interiors, which included the apartment for his newly married sister Hedwig and her husband, Karl Tedesko, followed the basic design concepts Strnad, Lurje, and Wlach were developing. Frank, though, would come to add his own touches, notably borrowings from the English designers (above all, C. F. A. Voysey and Mackay Hugh Baillie Scott). By 1912, his work also began to evince an even more pronounced paring down. Although Frank's first designs could not be called minimalist, they were often more austere than those of the others in the Strnad circle.[105]

In 1913, Frank and his Swedish-born wife, Anna (née Sebenius), moved into a large flat in a newly completed building designed by Arthur Baron, another graduate of the Technische Hochschule with whom Frank and Strnad were befriended. Frank deliberately chose the most "difficult" space in the building, the attic story. Because of the complex floor plan and the myriad angles created by the mansard roof, their suite of rooms was oddly shaped; almost all the spaces were nonorthogonal and some were unusually "composite."

Frank inserted into the higgledy-piggledy geometry a collection of pieces that were not dissimilar to those Strnad had been employing (a few of them, like the

Fig. 58| Josef Frank in his reserve officer uniform, 1913. Identification card for the Austria State Railways.
Fig. 59| Josef Frank, music and dining rooms, Josef and Anna Frank Apartment, Vienna 4., Wiedner Hauptstraße 64, 1913.

chairs in the dining area, *were* Strnad's), but they were much less conventionally positioned (figs. 59, 60). Indeed, Frank's solution is so striking because the furnishings almost seem to float in the space; they are wholly separated from the surrounding architectural frame—just as Strnad had suggested.

Nonetheless, it is not the imagery that is most important in Frank's design; rather it is his commentary about modern life. Many years afterward, Frank would repeatedly say and write that "modern is that which gives us freedom"—that it enables us to live as we wish, and the interiors (or the buildings themselves) should merely form a backdrop. They should never place demands on the inhabitants. Any piece of furniture or any decorative object could be added or taken away. There was no underlying concept to disturb because there was no concept other than to please and enable the lives of those who dwelled within.

In the coming years, after the war, Gorge and Frank would take the final step, to create spaces even less indebted to past forms. The first indication of this is visible in an interior Gorge designed just after the war (fig. 61).[106] It still retains the look and feel of the vernacular, but the old residue is gone. There is a new language of freshness and matter-of-factness.

The divide between the two competing visions of modernism at that time could not have been starker. On the one hand, there was the language of the new purism, filtered through the belief that stylistic uniformity should be the guiding idea—that modernism should look modern, that "functionalism" had a specific guise. The contrast between this and the alternative Strnad, Frank, and the others were presenting is splendidly evident in Otto Wagner's 1913 design for a room at a planned new hotel on the Ringstraße (fig. 62). Wagner's precisionist vision (which was derived in some respects from Hoffmann and Moser) would become the look of the *Neues Bauen* of the 1920s and 1930s. The Wiener Wohnkultur would open an entirely different path to modern living.[107]

After the war, Strnad gradually moved away from architecture and interior design, becoming more and more involved with theater—with the theaters themselves and with set designs. He died of a heart attack in 1935. He was only a few days short of his fifty-sixth birthday. Gorge would take a different path, turning increasingly to designing furnishings and other objects. He, too, died comparatively young, at the age of fifty-one. Frank and Wlach, now practicing without Strnad, would work together for many years. In 1925, with Sobotka, they would launch their own home furnishings and design shop, Haus & Garten. Sobotka soon dropped out, but for more than a decade, until the time of the "Anschluss," in 1938, the other two men would pursue and refine the elements of their new concept of living.[108]

In the wake of the brief 1934 civil war in Austria, Frank continued to promote the new Wohnkultur, but he would do so mostly in Stockholm, where he became the designer for the home furnishings shop Svenskt Tenn. For several years, Frank traveled back and forth between the cities, still carrying out commissions in Vienna.

Fig. 60| Josef Frank, living room, Josef and Anna Frank Apartment, 1913.
Fig. 61| Hugo Gorge, hall, before 1921.

Fig. 62| Otto Wagner, proposed guest room for the Hotel Wien on Karlsplatz, 1913.

After 1938, he settled permanently in Sweden. He lived there until his death in 1967, except for a several-years-long interruption in New York during World War II.

The Wiener Wohnkultur that Strnad, Frank, and the others devised in those six or seven years before 1914 would have a second life, in altered form, in the Swedish (later Scandinavian) Modern. It would become available around the globe in every IKEA store. Ingvar Kamprad, who founded IKEA in 1965, took away many ideas and forms from Svenkst Tenn, but his most profound and enduring contribution was to make them accessible by mass-producing them, something that Frank never did.[109]

The meanings of the Wiener Wohnkultur today are not only wrapped up with the ideas of informality and comfort. They are also about pluralism. A design ethos that is founded on the notion that very many forms and modes can have validity—that they can all be contemporary, whether old or new, whether stylistically related or not, whether they speak the same color language or have different surfaces and textures—is especially meaningful in our time. Such a design approach not only erases the old restrictions, but, as Frank claimed, it offers a sense of liberation. One can live and furnish as one will and still be "modern." The legacy of the Wiener Wohnkultur, however, yielded something more. By loosening the traditional strictures, by eradicating the artificiality of pure design, it opened for us a new living experience: moments of unmediated reality.

Appendix

"Wohnungs-Moden" (1907)

Adolf Loos

Published in the *Frankfurter Zeitung*, Zweites Morgenblatt, 8 December 1907, 1 (Feuilleton), 1–2.

Man spricht seit zwei Jahren von einem Bankerott der modernen Wohnungseinrichtungen. Man spricht davon, daß man wieder zu den alten Stilen zurückkehren solle. Und als letztes Heilmittel wird Biedermeyer verschrieben. In Deutschland hieß die moderne Bewegung Jugendstil. Bei uns Sezession. Beide Bezeichnungen sind Schimpfwörter geworden. Es sind bald zehn Jahre her, daß ich in einer Reihe von Artikeln vor diesen beiden Stilarten warnte. Ich sagte damals: Man möge sich weder in einer alten, noch in einer der neuen Stilarten einrichten, sondern modern. Mit meiner Ansicht blieb ich damals in der Minorität. In einer sehr kleinen Minorität sogar: Es war die Minoritätszahl eins. Unsere modernen Erzeugnisse wurden sowohl von den Künstlern, als auch von den staatlichen Behörden mit Geringschätzung behandelt. Ich verwies darauf, daß es doch gar nicht notwendig sei, den Stil unserer Zeit erst zu konstruieren, da wir ihn doch schon besitzen. Unsere Maschinen, unsere Kleidung, unsere Wagen und Pferdegeschirre, unsere Glas- und Metallwaren und alles, alles, was einer unzeitgemäßen Verballhornung durch die

Architekten entgangen war, war modern. Gewiß, die Tischlerarbeit war den Architekten seit 50 Jahren in Bausch und Bogen ausgeliefert. Es galt daher, sie von den Architektenwitzen und Kinkerlitzen zu befreien. Dann würde uns für die moderne Wohnungseinrichtung nichts mehr fehlen.

Der Weg hiezu war sehr einfach. Gewisse Erzeugnisse des Tischlers und Holzbearbeiters waren dem Architekten entgangen. Die hieß es nun zu sammeln und auf ähnliche Fälle zu verwenden. Da gab es Kassetten, die der Piccolo" in den Restaurants herumtrug, um die Zigarren zu servieren. Da gab es Eiskästen in den Kaffeehäusern für Gefrorenes. Da gab es Glasvitrinen in der Geschäfts-Einrichtungs--Branche. Da gab es Beschläge, Schlüsselbleche, die in der Kofferfabrikation verwendet wurden. Und sogar, wie sich die moderne Wandvertäfelung entwickelt hatte, konnte man erfahren: an den alten Waterclosets, die eine solche zur Verschalung des Wasserkastens und der Wand aufwiesen.

Nun hatte man die Tischlerarbeit. Aber dieser Tischlerarbeit fehlte das, was die Mitarbeit des Architekten zur Voraussetzung hatte, das Ornament. Da nämlich das alte Möbel geschnitzte oder eingelegte Ornamente und Profile aufwies, der moderne Tischler aber keine zeichnen kann, so drängte sich ihm der Architekt auf. Der Tischler kann das nicht, weil er ein moderner Mensch ist. Der Architekt konnte es und kann es, weil er ein unmoderner Mensch ist. Denn auch das behauptet ich vor zehn Jahren, daß ein moderner Mensch nicht mehr imstande ist ein Ornament hervorzubringen. Die modernen Erzeugnisse unserer Kultur weisen kein Ornament auf. Koffer- und Lederarbeiter, der Schneider, der Elektriker, der Maschinenfabrikant ornamentieren nicht. Nur Menschen, die wohl in der Gegenwart geboren, aber faktisch in einem früheren Jahrhunderte leben, die Frauen, die Landbevölkerung, die Orientalen (die Japaner mit eingeschlossen) und verstümmelte Hirne, wie die der Krawatten- und Tapetenmuster-Zeichner. Die bringen auch heute noch ein neues, dem alten Ornament gleich wertvolles hervor.

Das Unvermögen unserer Kultur, ein neues Ornament zu schaffen, bedeutet ihre Größe. Evolution der Menschheit geht Hand in Hand mit dem Entfernen des Ornamentes aus dem Gebrauchsgegenstande. Mögen unsere angewandten Künstler — aus Selbsterhaltungstrieb — einwenden, was sie wollen: Für den kultivierten Menschen ist ein nichttätowiertes Antlitz schöner, als ein tätowiertes und wenn die Tätowierung von Kolo Moser selber herrühren sollte. Und der Kulturmensch will nicht nur seine Haut, sondern auch seine Bucheinbände oder sein Nachtschränkchen von der indianischen Verzierungswut der staatlich angestellten Kulturbarbaren geschätzt wissen.

Das Ornament, das nicht organisch der menschlichen Seele entspringt, wie beim alten Meister, oder beim neuen Orientalen, ist wertlos. Wertlos, verlorene Arbeit, verschwendetes Material. Und diese Wertlosigkeit steigert sich von Tag zu Tag. Gebrauchsgegenstände, die noch vor fünf Jahren dem Käufer wertvoll erschienen, können heute kaum den zehnten Teil ihres Erstehungspreises bei Auktionen erzielen. Man täusche sich nicht: auch den Gegenständen, die nach der heutigen unkultivierten, daher unzeitgemässen, also unmodernen Richtung erzeugt werden, blüht in einigen Jahren dasselbe Schicksal.

Wir sollten trachten, bleibende Werte zu schaffen. Früher — es war die Zeit der grün, rot, violett und grau gebeizten Hölzer, die Zeit, wo jedes Möbel in einen Kreis gepresst wurde, oder große, aus Latten gebildete Kreise sich im Raume spannten —, da war wenigstens etwas zu spüren, was man meinetwegen angewandte Kunst nennen konnte. Jetzt müssen unsere Kanalgitter herhalten, den Dekor für Blumenvasen und Fruchtschalen zu liefern. Die Kultur hat ein Anrecht darauf, endlich vor den Experimentatoren Ruhe zu haben.

---

*) Adolf Loos hat sich bei der Bewegung um ein modernes Kunstgewerbe und die moderne Ausgestaltung unserer Heimstätten große Verdienste erworben. Wir geben daher gerne seinen Ausführungen Raum, ohne sie in allen Punkten uns zu eigen zu machen. D. Red.

"New Ways to Furnish Living Spaces" (1922)

Oskar Strnad

Originally published as "Neue Wege in der Wohnraum-Einrichtung," *Innen-Dekoration* 33 (October 1922): 323–28.

You have asked me to append a few words to accompany these images of my work.[1] This is more difficult for me than you might suppose. The older I get, the less I think about "problems." For me, designing is an inner challenge, a joy, a passion. The natural result of this passion is form. (My true longing is to create "form without form." Perhaps I will write about that some day). Thus, I can say hardly anything about my work. If I do make the attempt here to jot down a few thoughts that I have had while designing, it is because I believe that furniture and dwelling are less about aesthetics than they are a matter of "cultural decorum"—just like building houses! Still, I do have a few things to say. First: Keep the concepts of space and life apart! Space is destiny. Freeing yourself from it is making a path, delimiting space. So, not a wall, but a path, a floor. Keep the floor free and clear. Leave the floor edges visible. (The chair rail belongs to the floor, not to the wall.) Clear the corners (the joints of the room). Don't put anything in the corners. Develop the floor, let your body sense it. (You don't just see space, you feel it with your entire body, you hear and smell it.)

Enliven the room. Place flowerpots—right on the ground. Put down rugs. Not wall-to-wall carpets. Use many rugs, not just one. They enliven the space. Not factory-made carpets, they mean nothing. Not industrial work, just hand-made, beautiful, independent pieces. Make the walls feel as if they are wide apart. Don't build dungeons, but open worlds. The floor is a border, and the wall should be perceived as transparent and incorporeal. Don't subdivide the floors or walls; don't frame them. Wallpaper, with its repeats, makes a space seem smaller; it constricts the space. Paint the walls white. It makes the room seem bigger or ethereal. Or cover the wall, i.e., really dress it up. This covering should be hung, presented as something independent, something that does not belong to the room; it is like furniture, thus forming an independent "element." Cornices, frames, and wall divisions: treat them as surface, as a "tactile" experience, different from the incorporeal wall. Windows and doors are pathways into the distance; they are divisions of the space. Framing them gives them presence. Always make the frames visible; do not conceal them with draperies or textiles. Always hang the drapes from the inside of the frame. The ceiling, like the wall, should appear transparent, expanding the space; if it gives the impression of being weighty, it makes the room appear smaller.

Pieces of furniture should be placed independently of the room. They should merely exist in the space; they should be moveable, mobile (*Möbel*), with feet and their own existence (not as spatial element).[2] Never place furnishings in relation to the floor space. Furniture should have its own life and its own separate environment. Its physical presence is related to our bodies, to our own physicality, not to the surrounding space. It is ours. Its proportions are our own, not those of the room. Our relationship to space is the same as furniture. My relationship with room is reflected in it. Thus, do not make "architecture" with furniture, don't use it to organize the space. (Do not arrange the furnishings axially and avoid matched sets of furnishings!) Pieces of furniture should stand independently. Otherwise, they foster a sense of coercion, of servitude. Grasp that different pieces of furniture can coexist (different varieties of wood, different forms can exist in the same space). Express the organic nature of the furnishings, their vital, almost animate qualities, which are wholly independent of the floor. The surfaces of the room should feel like a skin, stretched so that one can sense their presence. Never allow the walls to become rigid. No cornices emerging from corners (reaching into the room). We should sense everything as if there is "tension from within." Otherwise, it would cease to be a "mobile," i.e., an independent thing. Above all, foster a direct relationship between the person and the space, that is: find the right scale! Everything that is too big, too voluminous should be avoided or banished from the living room. Textiles in the living room are its clothes, its ornament. So, never stretch them, always let them hang loose, put them on like clothes, cover the wall. Likewise with fabrics on the furniture: just put them on, never stretch them. Always allow the upholstery to hang loosely. Don't use "pillow" furniture. Furniture is [like a] bodily form, a fabric can never be a body, it is always merely a dress.

Fabrics live in space as free beings. Therefore, no matched sets, but individual elements, which means always use a variety of fabrics. Pure colors, no gold or silver, which give a sense of solidity, unlike a textile; no related patterns, which are coercive (so it is "architecture"). Ideally, only those textiles that are handwoven. No industrially produced textiles, they lack any character; use only those textiles that have the richness that comes from handwork.

Pictures in the living room are personalities; never use them to define space. Always hang them casually, randomly, without any spatial context (do not use them as an "axis"). Change them often. Do not "decorate" with pictures. Use only originals. Reproductions, including engravings, woodcuts, and lithographs, belong in a portfolio. Only real paintings have a connection to the room. Rooms have their own inner unity and tolerate nothing else in them. No built-in furniture. The human being is subject to artistic will and is an observer for the short period of time he is able to absorb what he experiences. Lamps are simply "bearers of light." Light itself is not capable of form. So only consider the form or the bearer. The modern light is the light bulb: a machine! It can never express spiritual things. Therefore, do not make them into "illuminating objects," nor should you create chandeliers with light bulbs. Do not use several lower wattage bulbs in place of a single, more powerful one. It should hang on a thin chain (do not let it hang on large cable), or it can be placed on a thin rod, a very light one. Never thicker than is necessary. To dim the glowing filament, use loose, soft, thin fabrics over the bulb. Make the shade as small as possible. Don't employ color fabrics to alter the color of the light, use only white fabrics. Always place light fixtures "randomly" in the room. Don't seek to create "architecture" with them. Use real, burning candles for special days.

The modern heater is also a machine. Make it as small as possible; don't make "form" with it. Partially encase it with bricks or ceramic tiles but leave the stove itself visible. Don't make a "modern" tiled stove. This is a form of romanticism, alien to us today; it never fits in. Don't install an old stove. Everything antiquarian is romantic; it is just a hobby, not real life; it undermines the rest of the design. Only what is truly inherited has the right to live.

When setting up the apartment: clarify your living needs; separate living and working spaces. A workspace is not living space, tools are not furniture. Never mix them up! (Office desks are impossible in the living room.) Above all, create "living rooms"—not "masters' rooms," "dining rooms," and "reception rooms." "Living" ultimately means "resting," i.e., sitting, lying down, or strolling about. Above all, employ a lot of armchairs (the sofa and bed are also a kind of "armchair"; make sure they are not boxes). Have many shapes in the same room, but make sure that they all make resting possible. Then add tables. But don't put them in the way. Leave the path free. Never place them in front of the sofa, always next to it. Allow every piece of furniture to stand freely. It is intended for the individual. Don't create "suites" of furniture! Make tables small (foldable), low (60 to 65 cm high), and make them light so that they can be put away without any bother. Otherwise, have only a few objects in the room and make these objects as small and light as possible. Always place them in such a way that they don't have a strong physical presence. (Each object should have its own "atmosphere.") Above all, keep the room "pure." Don't decorate it with pictures but with fabrics and flowers. Change these as often as possible because space must also "live."

This fundamental attitude toward space and form is a "cultural attitude." Once one grasps this idea, furnishing an apartment becomes a matter of course. . . .

---

[1] In the original version, Strnad's text accompanied six photographs of his interiors from just before and, possibly, immediately after the war. The next article in the magazine included photographs of the works of others "practicing" the Wiener Wohnkultur, including Frank. See K. H. [Karl Hoffmann], "Neu-Wiener Innenraum Kunst: Aus der Zuschrift einese Lesers," *Innen-Dekoration* 33 (October 1922): 331–34. Karl Hoffmann practiced with Felix Augenfeld, two other younger Viennese architects and designers following the lead of Strnad, Wlach, and Frank.

Anyone comparing my translation of this piece with the original will see that I have rendered Strnad's text quite freely. Strnad wrote in a highly idiosyncratic, almost poetic, language that loses its meaning in literal translation. I have sought to convey the sense of what he is saying, without producing a word-for-word version.

[2] The German word *Möbel* literally means that which is "mobile," i.e., which can be moved around. *Meubles*, in French, and *muebles,* in Spanish, carry the same meaning. Strnad here is also relying on the earlier Biedermeier concept that furnishings in a space could be constantly moved and rearranged for different activities. It was also common in the eighteenth century for pieces of furniture to be pushed against a wall when not in use. Strnad, however, rejects that idea, insisting that furniture should "float freely" in the space, not become "part of the architecture."

Notes

1| On Hevesi and his place in Vienna's art scene, see Ilona Sarmany-Parsons, *Die Macht der Kunstkritik: Ludwig Hevesi und die Wiener Moderne* (Göttingen: Vandenhoeck & Ruprecht, 2022).

2| Ludwig Hevesi, "Kunst auf der Straße," *Fremden-Blatt*, 30 May 1899, repr. in *Acht Jahre Sezession (März 1897–Juni 1905): Kritik–Polemik–Chronik* (Vienna: Carl Konegen, 1906), 174–75. He writes: "Als aufrichtiger Nichtsezessionist gibt sich Adolf Loos in seinem 'Café Museum.' Nicht als Feind der Wiener Sezession, aber als etwas anderes, denn modern sind schließlich beide." (Adolf Loos presents himself as a true non-Secessionist in his Café Museum. Not as an enemy of the Vienna Secession, but as something else, for both are modern.)

3| Ibid., 175.

4| Wilhelm Schölermann, "Die Wiener Richtung in der Innenraum-Ausstattung," *Innen-Dekoration* 16 (January 1905): 21.

5| Ibid., 38.

6| Ibid. Schölerman had already noted Loos's penchant for a radical simplicity several years before. In his review of Loos's Café Museum interiors, he was quite explicit about the "clarity" and "functionality" of Loos's spaces. Wilhem Schölermann, "Café Museum," *Wiener Rundschau* 12 (1898–99), repr. in *Kontroversen: Adolf Loos im Spiegel der Zeitgenossen*, ed. Adolf Opel (Vienna: Prachner, 1985), 9–10.

7| Ludwig Hevesi, "Biedermeier und Komp.," *Fremden-Blatt*, 29 November 1901, repr. in *Altkunst—Neukunst: Wien 1894–1908* (Vienna: Carl Konegen, 1909), 190.

8| "Dr. Charles Townsend," *Neues Wiener Tagblatt*, 30 January 1907, 11.

9| Classified advertisement in the *Neues Wiener Tagblatt*, 14 April 1907, 7.

10| Burkhardt Rukschcio and Roland Schachel, *Adolf Loos: Leben und Werk*, 2nd ed. (Salzburg and Vienna: Residenz, 1987), 109.

11| Ludwig Hevesi, "Gegen das moderne Ornament: Adolf Loos," *Fremden-Blatt*, 22 November 1907, 15–16, repr. in *Altkunst—Neukunst*, 286.

12| Ibid.

13| Ibid., 288.

14| Ibid., 285–86.

15| Ibid., 288.

16| Rukschcio and Schachel, *Adolf Loos*, 109.

17| Hevesi, *Altkunst—Neukunst*, 284.

18| Adolf Loos, *Wohnungswanderungen* (Vienna, 1907).

19| Rukschcio and Schachel, *Adolf Loos*, 110.

20| Ibid.

21| Ibid.

22| Adolf Loos, "Wohnungs-Moden," *Frankfurter Zeitung*, Zweites Morgenblatt, 8 December 1907, 1.

23| "Adolf Loos hat sich bei der Bewegung um ein modernes Kunstgewerbe und die moderne Ausgestaltung unserer Heimstätten große Verdienste erworben. Wir geben daher gerne seine Ausführungen Raum, ohne sie in allen Punkten uns zu eigen zu machen." Ibid.

24| See Christopher Long, "The Origins and Context of Adolf Loos's 'Ornament and Crime,'" *Journal of the Society of Architectural Historians* 68, no. 2 (June 2009): 200–223.

25| The exact phrase is "evolution der kultur ist gleichbedeutend mit dem entfernen des ornamentes aus dem gebrauchsgegenstande." Adolf Loos, "Ornament und Verbrechen," in *Trotzdem 1900–1930* (Innsbruck: Brenner, 1931), 82.

26| Loos, *Wohnungswanderungen*, n.p.

27| Ibid.

28| Charles Edouard Jeanneret, *Étude sur le mouvement d'art decoratif en Allemagne* (La Chaux-de-Fonds: Haefeli, 1912); Rukschcio and Schachel, *Adolf Loos*, 112.

29| B. Z. [Berta Zuckerkandl], "Kunst und Kultur: Wie es geworden ist," *Wiener Allgemeine Zeitung*, 14 December 1907, 5.

30| Rukschcio and Schachel, *Adolf Loos*, 113.

31| Plein-air [Adalbert Franz Seligmann], "Kunst," *Wiener Sonn- und Montags-Zeitung*, 27 July 1908, 2.

32| Ibid.

33| Ibid. Loos, in a handwritten note in the Loos Papers at the Albertina Museum, refers to Frank as "von mir hochgeschätzen Kollegen Dr. Frank" (my highly esteemed colleague Dr. Frank)—erroneously adding his later title since Frank had not yet finished his doctoral degree. See Rukschcio and Schachel, *Adolf Loos*, 114.

34| Adolf Loos, "Die Überflüssigen (Deutscher Werkbund)," *März: Halbmonatsschrift der deutsche Kultur* 2, no. 3 (3 August 1908): 185.

35| "Wir brauchen eine *Tischlerkultur*. Würden die angewandten Künstler wieder Bilder malen oder Straßen kehren, hätten wir sie." Ibid., 187.

36| "Redaktionelles," *März: Halbmonatsschrift der deutsche Kultur* 2, no. 3 (3 August 1908), 248.

37| Adolf Loos, "Lob der Gegenwart," *März: Halbmonatsschrift der deutsche Kultur* 2, no. 16 (18 August 1908): 310–12; and Adolf Loos, "Kultur," *März: Halbmonatsschrift*

der deutsche Kultur 2, no. 20 (18 October 1908): 134–36.
38| See Plein-air, "Kunst," 6.
39| On the planning and presentation of the exhibition, see Agnes Husslein-Arco and Alfred Weidinger, *Gustav Klimt und die Kunstschau 1908*, exh. cat. (Munich: Prestel, 2008).
40| On the role of the latter in the Kunstschau 1908, see Megan Brandow-Faller, *The Female Secession: Art and the Decorative at the Viennese Women's Academy* (University Park, PA: Pennsylvania State University Press, 2020), esp. 101–24.
41| See, e.g., Stanford Anderson, "The Legacy of German Neoclassicism and the Biedermeier," *Assemblage* 15 (August 1991): 67–87. One of the first to lay out the logic of reviving the architecture of the *Vormärz* was Hartwig Fischel, "Biedermeier als Vorbild," *Das Interieur* 2 (1901): 65–73. See also Joseph August Lux, "Biedermeier als Erzieher," *Hohe Warte* 1 (1904–5): 145–55; and Paul Mebes, ed., *Um 1800: Architektur und Handwerk im letzten Jahrhundert ihrer traditionellen Entwicklung*, 2 vols. (Munich: F. Bruckmann, 1908).
42| Eduard F. Sekler, *Josef Hoffmann: The Architectural Work; Monograph and Catalogue of Works* (Princeton, NJ: Princeton University Press, 1985), 119–20.
43| Loos, "Lob der Gegenwart," 310.
44| Loos, "Kultur," 136, repr. in *Trotzdem*, 66–69, quotation on 69.
45| Rukschcio and Schachel, *Adolf Loos*, 114–18.
46| Adolf Loos, "Kulturentartung," in *Trotzdem*, 74.
47| Ibid.
48| Ibid.
49| Alois Riegl, *Die spätrömische Kunst-Industrie nach den Funden in Österreich-Ungarn im Zusammenhange mit der Gesammtentwicklung der bildenden Künste bei den Mittelmeervölkern* (Vienna: K.K. Hof- und Staatsdruckerei, 1901).
50| Loos, "Kulturentartung," 76.
51| Ibid.
52| Ibid.
53| Ibid., 78.
54| Werner Sombart, *Kunstgewerbe und Kultur* (Berlin: Marquardt, 1908). On Sombart's critique, see also Joan Campbell, *The German Werkbund: The Politics of Reform in the Applied Arts* (Princeton, NJ: Princeton University Press, 1978), 30–31.
55| Joseph August Lux, *Otto Wagner* (Munich: Delphin, 1914); and Joseph August Lux, *Joseph Maria Olbrich* (Berlin: Ernst Wasmuth, 1919). On Lux's design writings, see, e.g., Joseph August Lux, *Die moderne Wohnung und Ihre Ausstattung* (Vienna: Wiener Verlag, 1905); and Joseph August Lux, *Der Geschmack im Alltag: Ein Buch zur Pflege des Schönen* (Dresden: Kühtmann, 1908).
56| Mark Jarzombek, "Joseph August Lux: Werkbund Promoter, Historian of a Lost Modernity," *Journal of the Society of Architectural Historians* 63, no. 2 (June 2004): 202–4.
57| See Joseph August Lux, "Der 'Deutsche Werkbund,'" *Der Kunstwart* 21, no. 4 (November 1907): 270–72.
58| Joseph August Lux, *Das neue Kunstgewerbe in Deutschland* (Leipzig: Klinkhardt & Biermann, 1908), 241.
59| Ibid., 249.

60| For a brilliant reading of the ornamental craze, its sources, and its expressions, see Lada Hubatová-Vacková, *Silent Revolutions in Ornament: Studies in Applied Arts and Crafts from 1880–1930* (Prague: Academy of Arts, Architecture, and Design, 2011).

61| Ibid., 218. The pattern book in question was Josef Ritter von Storck, *Die Pflanze in der Kunst: Ein Vorlagenwerk für den Zeichenunterricht und Kunstgewerbe, ein Anschauungs-mittel für ornamentale Stillehre, ein Nachschlagebuch für Künstler und Kunsthandwerker* (Vienna: R. V. Waldheim, [ca. 1880]).

62| On the genesis of the essay and its dating, see Long, "Origins and Context."

63| On the larger ornament debate in Germany, see María Ocón Fernández, *Ornament und Moderne: Theoriebildung und Ornamentdebatte im deutschen Architekturdiskurs (1850–1930)* (Berlin: Dietrich Reimer, 2004); and Gérard Raulet and Burghart Schmidt, eds., *Kritische Theorie des Ornaments* (Berlin: Dietrich Reimer, 2004). For a treatment of the narrower Viennese context, see Rainald Franz, "Josef Hoffmann and Adolf Loos: The Ornament Controversy in Vienna," in *Josef Hoffmann Designs*, ed. Peter Noever (Munich: Prestel, 1992), 11–15.

64| Karl Widmer, "Die Karlsruher Jubiläums-Ausstellung für Kunst und Kunstgewerbe," *Deutsche Kunst und Dekoration* 19 (October 1906–March 1907): 132.

65| Joseph August Lux, "Die Erneuerung der Ornamentik," *Innen-Dekoration* 18 (1907): 291.

66| See, for example, Hermann Muthesius, "M. H. Baillie Scott – Bedford," *Deutsche Kunst und Dekoration* 19 (October 1906–March 1907): 430. Muthesius writes, quoting Scott, "better no ornament than that from an inartistic hand."

67| Robert Breuer, "Das Leben im Gerät," *Deutsche Kunst und Dekoration* 20 (April–September 1907): 210.

68| Richard Schaukal, "Gegen das Ornament," *Deutsche Kunst und Dekoration* 22 (April 1908): 12–13, 15.

69| Schaukal writes: "Ein Tüchtiger hat schon vor Jahren den Kampf gegen das willkürliche Ornament aufgenommen: Adolf Loos, ein Wiener Architekt. Ihm ist die Lösung: 'Los vom Ornament!' eine Glaubens- und Gewissenssache. Er sieht in der ornamentlosen Zukunft, die er erträumt, die Menschheit von einem Fluch befreit, sieht nutzlose Arbeit abgetan, die Produktion vereinfacht, den Gewinn, zumal der Handwerker, mit geringern Mitteln erzielbar." Ibid.

70| Richard Schaukal, "Adolf Loos: Geistige Landschaft mit vereinzelter Figur im Vordergrund," *Innen-Dekoration* 19 (August 1908): 252, 254, 256–57, 259. The piece was later reprinted in Herwarth Walden's little magazine *Der Sturm*. See *Der Sturm* 13 (26 May 1910): 101–2.

71| Schaukal, "Adolf Loos," 257.

72| Ibid., 257, 59.

73| Wilhelm Michel, "Die Schicksale des Ornaments," *Innen-Dekoration* 20 (July 1909): 232. Another writer, Hamburg journalist and architecture critic Paul Bröcker, made an even more assertive defense of ornament, claiming, "Die Schmuckform ist . . . die höchste Zweckform eines Gebrauchgegenstandes"—that in essence ornamental forms and the expression of utility could not be separated from one another in objects of daily use. See Paul Bröcker, "Über das Wesen des Ornaments," *Deutsche Kunst und Dekoration* 19 (October 1906–March 1907): 57.

74| Georg Simmel, "Das Probleme des Stiles," *Dekorative Kunst* 11 (April 1908): 310.

75| Iris Meder, "Oskar Strnad—Immer bestimmend ist nur der Mensch," in *Oskar Strnad 1879–1935*, by Iris Meder and Evi Fuchs, exh. cat. (Vienna: Jüdisches Museum der Stadt Wien; Salzburg: Anton Pustet, 2007), 10. On Strnad's life and work, see also Max Eisler, *Oskar Strnad* (Vienna: Gerlach und Weidling, 1936); Joseph Gregor, *Rede auf Oskar Strnad* (Vienna: H. Reicher, 1936); Otto Niedermoser, *Oskar Strnad 1879–1935* (Vienna: Bergland, 1935); Juliane Stoklaska, "Oskar Strnad" (PhD diss., Universität Wien, 1960); Johannes Spalt and Manfred Wagner, eds., *Der Architekt Oskar Strnad zum hundertsten Geburtstag am 26. Oktober 1979*, exh. cat. (Vienna: Hochschule für angewandte Kunst, 1979); Ulla Weich, "Die theoretischen Ansichten des Architekten und Lehrers Oskar Strnad" (Diplomarbeit, Universität Wien, 1995); and Ursula Prokop, "Oskar Strnad," Architektenlexikon, Architekturzentrum Wien, accessed 12 January 2024, https://www.architektenlexikon.at/de/635.htm.

76| Meder, "Oskar Strnad," 11.

77| Oskar Strnad, "Das Princip der Dekoration in der frühchristlichen Kunst" (PhD diss., Technische Hochschule Wien, 1904).

78| On Wlach's life and career, see Ursula Prokop, "Oskar Wlach," Architektenlexikon, Architekturzentrum Wien, accessed 1 February 2024, https://www.architektenlexikon.at/de/695.htm. See also Christopher Long, "Refuge and Respite: The Wiener Wohnkultur and the Culture of the Modern Jewish Interior," in *Designing Transformation: Jews and Cultural Identity in Central European Modernism*, ed. Elana Shapira (London: Bloomsbury, 2021), 157–71.

79| On Viktor Lurje, see Ursula Prokop, "Viktor Lurje," Architektenlexikon, Architekturzentrum Wien, accessed 1 February 2024, https://www.architektenlexikon.at/de/1437.htm.

80| Meder, "Oskar Strnad," 11.

81| See Christopher Long, *The New Space: Movement and Experience in Viennese Modern Architecture* (New Haven and London: Yale University Press, 2016).

82| Its official name was the Verein des Kaiser-Franz-Josef-Jubiläums-See-Hospiz. It was located in Palais Bauer, Türkenstraße 17, in the ninth district.

83| Nikolaus Pevsner, *Pioneers of Modern Design* (London: Penguin Books, 1964), 152.

84| Anthony Alofsin, "The Kunsthistorisches Museum: A Treasure House for the Secessionists," *Jahrbuch der Kunsthistorischen Sammlungen in Wien* 88 (1992): 190.

85| *Ausstellung Österreichischer Kunstgewerbe 1910–1911*, exh. cat. (Vienna: K.k. Österreichisches Museum für Kunst und Industrie, 1910), 3. On the full exhibition, see Sabine Forsthuber, *Moderne Raumkunst: Wiener Ausstellungsbauten von 1898 bis 1914* (Vienna: Picus, 1991), 150–51.

86| Forsthuber, *Moderne Raumkunst*, 152.

87| *Ausstellung Österreichischer Kunstgewerbe 1911–1912*, exh. cat. (Vienna: K.k. Österreichisches Museum für Kunst und Industrie, 1911), 8.

88| For a discussion of the exhibition and its import, see Christopher Long, "Wiener Wohnkultur: Interior Design in Vienna, 1910–1938," *Studies in the Decorative Arts* 5 (Fall–Winter 1997–98): 29–51.

89| On the founding of the Austrian Werkbund and its later history, see Astrid Gmeiner and Gottfried Pirhofer, eds., *Der Österreichische Werkbund: Alternative zur klassischen Moderne in Architektur, Raum- und Produktgestaltung* (Salzburg and Vienna: Residenz, 1985).

90| Adolf Loos, "Vom armen reichen Mann," *Neues Wiener Tagblatt*, 26 April 1900, 1–2.
91| The lectures took place on 31 March and 7 and 14 April 1914. "Brautkurse 1914," *Urania: Wochenschrift für Volksbildung* 7, no. 11–13 (28 March 1914): 88; no. 14 (4 April 1914): 104; and no. 15 (11 April 1914): 120.
92| Meder and Fuchs, *Oskar Strnad 1879–1935*, 114.
93| In the Urania's schedule, the lectures are listed under "Brautkurse," courses for brides. Undoubtedly others attended, but it is likely that most who signed up were younger women.
94| Oskar Strnad, "Von der Anlage der Wohnung," typescript of a lecture presented at the Vienna Urania on 31 March 1914, repr. in Meder and Fuchs, *Oskar Strnad 1879–1935*, 107.
95| Oskar Strnad, "Vom Licht, vom Besteck und Geschirr, von den Stoffen und Teppichen, also auch vom Ornament," typescript of a lecture presented at the Vienna Urania, 14 April 1914, repr. in Meder and Fuchs, *Oskar Strnad 1879–1935*, 119–20.
96| Oskar Strnad, "Neue Wege in der Wohnraum-Einrichtung," *Innen-Dekoration* 33 (October 1922): 323–28.
97| Ibid., 323–24.
98| On Sobotka's life and career, see Ursula Prokop, "Walter Sobotka," Architektenlexikon, Architekturzentrum Wien, accessed 25 January 2024, https://www.architektenlexikon.at /de/612.htm.
99| Max Eisler, "Die schöne Wohnung," *Das Zelt: Eine jüdische illustrierte Monatsschrift* 1, no. 3 (1924): 106, 108. See also Evelyn Adunka, *Max Eisler, Wiener Kunsthistoriker und Publizist zwischen orthodoxer Lebenspraxis, sozialem Engagement und wissenschaftlicher Exzellenz* (Berlin: Hentrich & Hentrich, 2018).
100| Otto Niedermoser, "Oskar Strnad Gedächtnisausstellung, 10. Mai bis 22. Juni 1968, Akademie für angewandte Kunst: Pressemappe," typescript, n.p. Collection Christopher Long.
101| "Strnad war niemals provokant; er verstand und erstrebte es immer, seine Ideen so selbstverständlich, so unauffällig zu servieren, daß sie für den oberflächlichen Betrachter kaum auffielen. Er war ein Revolutionär der Stille." Ibid.
102| On Frank's early life and education, see Christopher Long, *Josef Frank: Life and Work* (Chicago and London: University of Chicago Press, 2002): esp. chapter 1.
103| Claudia Mazanek recently discovered that Frank and Broch lived in the same building, the so-called Pollak or Gotisches-Haus (1863–66), at Gölsdorfgasse 4, designed by Heinrich Ferstel. Claudia Mazanek, email to the author, 26 January 2024.
104| Josef Frank, "Über die ursprüngliche Gestalt der Kirchenbauten des Leone Battista Alberti" (PhD diss., Technische Hochschule Wien, 1910). See also Caterina Cardamone, *Josef Frank: L'architettura religiosa di Leon Battista Alberti* (Milan: Mondadori Electa, 2018).
105| Oskar Wlach, in an early article about his friend Frank, specifically refers to a circle "around Oskar Strnad and Viktor Lurje." Strnad, though, was a more dominant figure than Lurje, who soon moved on to other pursuits. Oskar Wlach, "Zu den Arbeiten Josef Franks," *Das Interieur* 13, no. 6 (1912): 41. On Frank and the others, see Ursula Prokop, "Josef Frank and 'The Small Circle around Oskar Strnad and Viktor Lurje': The Problem of Josef Frank's and His Colleagues' Jewish Identity," in *Josef Frank: Against Design; Das anti-formalistiche Werk des Architekten*, ed. Christoph Thun-Hohenstein, Hermann

Czech, and Sebastian Hackenschmidt, exh. cat. (Basel: Birkhäuser Verlag; Vienna: MAK–Museum für angewandte Kunst, 2016), 49.

106| Hugo Gorge (1883–1934) was born in Butovice, a small town in Moravia. After completing his studies at the Technische Hochschule in Vienna, he worked briefly for Friedrich Ohmann and was Strnad's assistant at the Kunstgewerbeschule for a year. Just before the war, he designed an apartment building at Laimgrubengasse 4, but for much of his early career he designed individual furnishings. Later, in the 1920s, he worked on several of the large communal housing projects in Vienna. At the same time, his role in the Wiener Wohnkultur faded. See Inge Scheidl, "Hugo Gorge," Architektenlexikon, Architekturzentrum Wien, accessed 31 January 2024, https://www.architektenlexikon.at/de/178.htm.

107| On the development of the Wiener Wohnkultur after the war and its import, see the excellent book by Michelle Jackson-Beckett, *Vienna and the New Wohnkultur, 1918–1938* (Oxford: Oxford University Press, 2024).

108| On Haus & Garten, see Marlene Ott-Wodni, *Josef Frank 1885–1967: Raumgestaltung und Möbeldesign*, Publikationsreihe der Museen des Mobiliendepots, Band 33 (Vienna: Böhlau, 2015); and Martina Wallner, *Haus & Garten–Frank & Wlach: Ein Beitrag zur österreichischen Wohnkultur* (Graz: Technische Universität Graz, [2009]).

109| On the role of the Wiener Wohnkultur in the making of IKEA, see Rebecca Carrai, "IKEA-LAND: A Counter-History of Domestic Space" (PhD diss., KU Leuven, 2023), esp. chapter 3.

Acknowledgments

Even relatively short books like this one require the work of many minds and hands. I am deeply grateful to the archivists and librarians who aided me with this project: Jack Glover at the Victoria & Albert Museum, London; Alice Hundsdorfer-Zhou, at the Albertina Museum; Thomas Matyk, at the Museum für angewandte Kunst, Vienna; and Maximilian Zauner at the Wien Museum, Vienna. I owe a special debt of thanks to Wolfgang Thaler, who made the photograph of Oskar Strnad and Oskar Wlach's 1911 Hörandner apartment building on the Stuckgasse, in Vienna, and to Magdalena Kokešová, who prepared and enhanced some of the images.

I also owe a debt to my colleagues in Austria and the United States, with whom I have had many discussions over the years that sharpened my understanding of Viennese modernism. I would especially like to thank Bernadette Reinhold and Gerd Ziller, who exemplify the best of art scholarship in our time. Working with Michelle Jackson-Beckett on her dissertation (and now book) on the later Wiener Wohnkultur brought home for me many of the questions I engage in this book.

I was fortunate to collaborate once more with Florence Grant, one of the very best editors I have had the privilege to work with, who made many small changes and corrections that greatly improved the text. I am grateful to Karel Kerlicý at Kant, who took this project on and shepherded it through the publication. I also owe a very large debt of thanks to Jiří Příhoda, who designed and laid out the book, and supervised its printing.

As always, I was aided by my very smart wife Gia Maria Houck, who has a keen eye for language and clarity of meaning. She always knows what I want to say.

The Martin S. Kermacy Centennial Professorship paid for the images in this book and for some of the costs of production. Martin was a lovely man, and I am pleased to honor his legacy with another book.

I especially wish to acknowledge a friend and colleague with whom I have now worked on many publications. Claudia Mazanek went through the book manuscript fastidiously, spotting inconsistencies in the text or errors in German and effectively fact-checking the whole. She has been a boon not only to those of us writing about Josef Frank, but to nearly everyone engaged with the history of the *Wiener Moderne*. Her services to the field have been legion, and it would be impossible to overstate the value of her contributions over many years.

Select Bibliography

Archival Sources

Albertina Museum, Vienna

MAK–Museum für angewandte Kunst, Vienna

Österreichische Nationalbibliothek, Bildarchiv, Vienna

Universität für angewandte Kunst—Sammlung, Vienna

Wienbibliothek im Rathaus, Vienna

Wien Museum, Vienna

Primary Sources

Ausstellung Österreichischer Kunstgewerbe 1910–1911. Exh. cat. Vienna: K.k. Österreichisches Museum für Kunst und Industrie, 1910.

Ausstellung Österreichischer Kunstgewerbe 1911–1912. Exh. cat. Vienna: K.k. Österreichisches Museum für Kunst und Industrie, 1911.

Blei, Fritz. "Die Wiener Werkstätte." *Deutsche Kunst und Dekoration* 19 (October 1906–March 1907): 37–45.

Breuer, Robert. "Das Leben im Gerät." *Deutsche Kunst und Dekoration* 20 (April–September 1907): 208–10.

Bröcker, Paul. "Über das Wesen des Ornaments." *Deutsche Kunst und Dekoration* 19 (October 1906–March 1907): 54–60.

B. Z. [Berta Zuckerkandl]. "Kunst und Kultur: Wie es geworden ist." *Wiener Allgemeine Zeitung*, 14 December 1907, 4–5.

"Dr. Charles Townsend." *Neues Wiener Tagblatt*, 30 January 1907, 11.

Eisler, Max. "Die schöne Wohnung." *Das Zelt: Eine jüdische illustrierte Monatsschrift* 1, no. 3 (1924): 106, 108.

———. *Oskar Strnad*. Vienna: Gerlach und Wiedling, 1936.

———. *Österreichische Werkkultur*. Vienna: Anton Schroll, 1916.

Fischel, Hartwig. "Biedermeier als Vorbild." *Das Interieur* 2 (1901): 65–73.

Frank, Josef. "Über die ursprüngliche Gestalt der Kirchenbauten des Leone Battista Alberti." PhD diss., Technische Hochschule Wien, 1910.

Gregor, Joseph. *Rede auf Oskar Strnad*. Vienna: H. Reicher, 1936.

Hevesi, Ludwig. *Acht Jahre Secession (März 1897–Juni 1905): Kritik—Polemik—Chronik*. Vienna: Carl Konegen, 1906.

———. *Altkunst—Neukunst: Wien 1894–1908*. Vienna: Carl Konegen, 1909.

Hoffmann, Josef. "Einfache Möbel." *Das Interieur* 2 (1901): 194–208.

Jeanneret, Charles Edouard. *Étude sur le mouvement d'art decoratif en Allemagne*. La Chaux-de-Fonds: Haefeli, 1912.

Knoll, Carl, and Fritz Reuther. *Die Kunst des Schmückens: Eine Klärung des Schmuck-problems durch Wort und Bild für Schaffende und Genießende*. Dresden: Gerhard Kühtmann, 1910.

Kulka, Heinrich. *Adolf Loos: Das Werk des Architekten*. Vienna: Anton Schroll, 1931.

Loos, Adolf. "Die Überflüssigen (Deutscher Werkbund)." *März: Halbmonatsschrift der deutsche Kultur* 2, no. 3 (3 August 1908): 185–87.

———. *Ins Leere gesprochen 1897–1900*. Paris: Éditions G. Crès et Cie, 1921.

———. "Kultur." *März: Halbmonatsschrift der deutsche Kultur* 2, no. 20 (18 October 1908): 134–36.

———. "Lob der Gegenwart." *März: Halbmonatsschrift der deutsche Kultur* 2, no. 16 (18 August 1908): 310–12.

———. *Trotzdem 1900–1930*. Innsbruck: Brenner, 1931.

———. "Vom armen reichen Mann." *Neues Wiener Tagblatt*, 26 April 1900, 1–2. Reproduced in *Der Sturm* 1, no. 1 (3 March 1910): 4.

———. "Vom Gehen, Stehen, Sitzen, Liegen, Schlafen, Essen, Trinken." *Der Sturm* 2, no. 87 (November 1911): 691–92.

———. “Wohnungs-Moden.” *Frankfurter Zeitung,* Zweites Morgenblatt, 8 December 1907, 1.

———. *Wohnungswanderungen*. Vienna, 1907.

Lux, Joseph August. “Biedermeier als Erzieher.” *Hohe Warte* 1 (1904–5): 145–55.

———. *Das neue Kunstgewerbe in Deutschland*. Leipzig: Klinkhardt & Biermann, 1908.

———. “Der ‘Deutsche Werkbund.’” *Der Kunstwart* 21, no. 4 (November 1907): 270–72.

———. *Der Geschmack im Alltag: Ein Buch zur Pflege des Schönen*. Dresden: Kühtmann, 1908.

———. “Die Erneuerung der Ornamentik.” *Innen-Dekoration* 18 (1907): 286–92, 352–54.

———. “Die Kunst des Tischlers.” *Das Interieur* 10 (1909): 5–11, 13–20, 23–24.

———. *Die moderne Wohnung und ihre Ausstattung.* Vienna: Wiener Verlag, 1905.

———. *Joseph Maria Olbrich*. Berlin: Ernst Wasmuth, 1919.

———. *Otto Wagner*. Munich: Delphin, 1914.

Mebes, Paul, ed. *Um 1800: Architektur und Handwerk im letzten Jahrhundert ihrer traditionellen Entwicklung*. 2 vols. Munich: F. Bruckmann, 1908.

Michel, Wilhelm. “Die Schicksale des Ornaments.” *Innen-Dekoration* 20 (1909): 231–37.

———. “Neue Tendenzen im Kunstgewerbe.” *Innen-Dekoration* 21 (1910): 127–28, 135.

Muthesius, Hermann. “M. H. Baillie Scott – Bedford.” *Deutsche Kunst und Dekoration* 19 (October 1906–March 1907): 423–31.

“Nach Entwürfen des Architekten Adolf Loos . . .” *Neues Wiener Tagblatt*, 14 April 1907, 7.

Opel, Adolf, ed. *Kontroversen: Adolf Loos im Spiegel der Zeitgenossen*. Vienna: Prachner, 1985.

Oppenheimer, Max. “Gegen die Mode.” *Das Interieur* 11 (1910): 85, 88.

Plein-air [Adalbert Franz Seligmann]. “Kunst.” *Wiener Sonn- und Montags-Zeitung*, 27 July 1908, 2.

Pudor, Heinrich. “Die Zweckform der Möbel.” *Das Interieur* 11 (1910): 49–51.

Riegl, Alois. *Die spätrömische Kunst-Industrie nach den Funden in Österreich-Ungarn im Zusammenhange mit der Gesammtentwicklung der bildenden Künste bei den Mittelmeervölkern.* Vienna: K.K. Hof- und Staatsdruckerei, 1901.

Schaukal, Richard. “Adolf Loos: Geistige Landschaft mit vereinzelter Figur im Vordergrund.” *Innen-Dekoration* 19 (August 1908): 252, 254, 256–57, 259. Reproduced in *Der Sturm* 13 (26 May 1910): 101–2.

———. “Gegen das Ornament.” *Deutsche Kunst und Dekoration* 22 (April 1908): 12–13, 15.

———. *Vom Geschmack*. Munich: Georg Müller, 1910.

Scheffers, Otto. "Zweckform und Ornament." *Deutsche Kunst und Dekoration* 24 (1909): 234–38.

Scheu, Robert. "Adolf Loos." *Die Fackel* 11, nos. 283–84 (26 June 1909): 25–37.

Schölermann, Wilhelm. "Die Wiener Richtung in der Innenraum-Ausstattung." *Innen-Dekoration* 16 (January 1905): 19, 21, 23, 26–28, 33, 38–40.

Schulze-Eberfeld, Otto. "Über Ornament-Symbolik." *Innen-Dekoration* 21 (1910): 378–87.

Sokal, Max. "Von Zierkunst und Arbeit." *Sozialistische Monatshefte* 2 (1912): 1055–59.

Sombart, Werner. *Kunstgewerbe und Kultur*. Berlin: Marquardt, 1908.

Storck, Josef Ritter von. *Die Pflanze in der Kunst: Ein Vorlagenwerk für den Zeichenunterricht und Kunstgewerbe, ein Anschauungsmittel für ornamentale Stillehre, ein Nachschlagebuch für Künstler und Kunsthandwerker*. Vienna: R. V. Waldheim, [ca. 1880].

Strnad, Oskar. "Das Princip der Dekoration in der frühchristlichen Kunst." PhD diss., Technische Hochschule Wien, 1904.

———. "Neue Wege in der Wohnraum-Einrichtung." *Innen-Dekoration* 33 (October 1922): 323–28.

———. "Vom Licht, vom Besteck und Geschirr, von den Stoffen und Teppichen, also auch vom Ornament." Typescript of a lecture presented at the Vienna Urania, 14 April 1914. Reproduced in Meder and Fuchs, *Oskar Strnad 1879–1935*, 119–20.

———. "Von den Möbeln, vom Stellen der Möbel, etc." Typescript of a lecture presented at the Vienna Urania, 7 April 1914.

———. "Von der Anlage der Wohnung." Typescript of a lecture presented at the Vienna Urania, 31 March 1914. Reproduced in Meder and Fuchs, *Oskar Strnad 1879–1935*, 107.

Thun-Hohenstein, Christoph, Hermann Czech, and Sebastian Hackenschmidt, eds. *Josef Frank: Against Design; Das anti-formalistiche Werk des Architekten*. Exh. cat. Basel: Birkhäuser; Vienna: MAK–Museum für angewandte Kunst, 2016.

Vischer, Franz Theodor. "Einiges über das Ornament." *Das Interieur* 12 (1911): 49.

———. "Warum wir keinen künstlerischen Stil haben." *Das Interieur* 12 (1911): 47.

Widmer, Karl. "Die Karlsruher Jubiläums-Ausstellung für Kunst und Kunstgewerbe." *Deutsche Kunst und Dekoration* 19 (October 1906–March 1907): 125–35.

Wlach, Oskar. "Zu den Arbeiten Josef Franks." *Das Interieur* 13, no. 6 (1912): 41–48.

"Wohnungswanderungen." *Arbeiter Zeitung*, 8 December 1907, 9.

"Wohnungswanderungen." *Illustrirtes Wiener Extrablatt*, 5 December 1907, 8.

"Wohnungswanderungen." *Wiener Allgemeine Zeitung*, 4 December 1907, 3.

Secondary Sources

Alofsin, Anthony. "The Kunsthistorisches Museum: A Treasure House for the Secessionists." *Jahrbuch der Kunsthistorischen Sammlungen in Wien* 88 (1992): 189–203.

Anderson, Stanford. "The Legacy of German Neoclassicism and the Biedermeier." *Assemblage* 15 (August 1991): 67–87.

Asenbaum, Paul, Stefan Asenbaum, and Christian Witt-Dörring, eds. *Moderne Vergangenheit: Wien 1800–1900*. Exh. cat. Vienna: Künstlerhaus, 1981.

Brandow-Faller, Megan. *The Female Secession: Art and the Decorative at the Viennese Women's Academy*. University Park, PA: Pennsylvania State University Press, 2020.

Campbell, Joan. *The German Werkbund: The Politics of Reform in the Applied Arts*. Princeton, NJ: Princeton University Press, 1978.

Cardamone, Caterina. *Josef Frank: L'architettura religiosa di Leon Battista Alberti*. Milan: Mondadori Electa, 2018.

Carrai, Rebecca. "IKEA-LAND: A Counter-History of Domestic Space." PhD diss., KU Leuven, 2023.

Fernández, María Ocón. *Ornament und Moderne: Theoriebildung und Ornamentdebatte im deutschen Architekturdiskurs (1850–1930)*. Berlin: Dietrich Reimer, 2004.

Forsthuber, Sabine. *Moderne Raumkunst: Wiener Ausstellungsbauten von 1898 bis 1914*. Vienna: Picus, 1991.

Franz, Rainald. "Josef Hoffmann and Adolf Loos: The Ornament Controversy in Vienna." In *Josef Hoffmann Designs*, edited by Peter Noever, 11–15. Munich: Prestel, 1992.

Gmeiner, Astrid, and Gottfried Pirhofer, eds. *Der Österreichische Werkbund: Alternative zur klassischen Moderne in Architektur, Raum- und Produktgestaltung*. Salzburg and Vienna: Residenz, 1985.

Haiko, Peter, and Mara Reissberger, "Quelques Réflexions à propos du débat sur l'ornement entre 1900 et 1910." In *Critique de l'ornement de Vienne à la postmodernité*, edited by Michel Collomb and Gérard Raulet, 123–31. Paris: Méridien-Klincksieck, 1992.

Hanisch, Ruth. *Moderne vor Ort: Wiener Architektur 1889–1938*. Vienna: Böhlau, 2018.

Hubatová-Vacková, Lada. *Silent Revolutions in Ornament: Studies in Applied Arts and Crafts from 1880–1930*. Prague: Academy of Arts, Architecture, and Design, 2011.

Jackson-Beckett, Michelle. *Vienna and the New Wohnkultur, 1918–1938*. Oxford: Oxford University Press, 2024.

Jarzombek, Mark. "Joseph August Lux: Werkbund Promoter, Historian of a Lost Modernity." *Journal of the Society of Architectural Historians* 63, no. 2 (June 2004): 202–19.

Kristan, Markus. *Adolf Loos: Villen*. Vienna: Album, 2001.

———. *Adolf Loos: Wohnungen*. Vienna: Album, 2001.

———. *Josef Hoffmann: Bauten & Interieurs*. Vienna: Album, 2002.

———. *Villenkolonie Hohe Warte*. Vienna: Album: 2004.

Künstler, Gustav. "Der 'Traditionalist' Adolf Loos." *Österreichische Zeitschrift für Kunst und Denkmalpflege* 22, no. 2 (1968): 83–90.

Long, Christopher. "Adolf Loos and the Biedermeier Revival in Vienna." *Centropa* 10, no. 2 (May 2010): 128–40.

———. *Essays on Adolf Loos*. Prague: Kant, 2019.

———. *Josef Frank: Life and Work*. Chicago and London: University of Chicago Press, 2002.

———. *The New Space: Movement and Experience in Viennese Modern Architecture*. New Haven and London: Yale University Press, 2016.

———. "The Origins and Context of Adolf Loos's 'Ornament and Crime.'" *Journal of the Society of Architectural Historians* 68, no. 2 (June 2009): 200–223.

———. "Refuge and Respite: The Wiener Wohnkultur and the Culture of the Modern Jewish Interior." In *Designing Transformation: Jews and Cultural Identity in Central European Modernism*, edited by Elana Shapira, 157–71. London: Bloomsbury, 2021.

———. "Wiener Wohnkultur: Interior Design in Vienna, 1910–1938." *Studies in the Decorative Arts* 5 (Fall–Winter 1997–98): 29–51.

Meder, Iris, and Evi Fuchs. *Oskar Strnad, 1879–1935*. Exh. cat. Vienna: Jüdisches Museum der Stadt Wien; Salzburg: Anton Pustet, 2007.

Mitterer, Cornelius. *Richard Schaukal im Netzwerken und Feldern der literarischen Moderne*. Berlin and Boston: De Gruyter, 2020.

Niedermoser, Otto. *Oskar Strnad 1879–1935*. Vienna: Bergland, 1935.

Ottillinger, Eva B. *Adolf Loos: Wohnkonzepte und Möbelentwürfe*. Salzburg: Residenz, 1994.

Ott-Wodni, Marlene. *Josef Frank, 1885–1967: Raumgestaltung und Möbeldesign*. Publikationsreihe der Museen des Mobiliendepots, Band 33. Vienna: Böhlau, 2015.

Pevsner, Nikolaus. *Pioneers of Modern Design*. London: Penguin Books, 1964.

Podbrecky, Inge, and Rainald Franz, eds. *Leben mit Loos*. Vienna: Böhlau, 2008.

Posch, Wilfried. "Der Streit um Alt und Neu: Adolf Loos." In *Das grössere Österreich: Geistiges und soziales Leben von 1880 bis zur Gegenwart*, edited by Kristian Sotriffer, 182–87. Vienna: Edition Tusch, 1982.

Prokop, Ursula. "Oskar Strnad." Architektenlexikon, Architekturzentrum Wien. Accessed 12 January 2024. https://www.architektenlexikon.at/de/635.htm.

———. "Oskar Wlach." Architekenlexikon, Architekturzentrum Wien. Accessed 1 February 2024. https://www.architektenlexikon.at/de/695.htm.

———. "Viktor Lurje." Architektenlexikon, Architekturzentrum Wien. Accessed 1 February 2024. https://www.architektenlexikon.at/de/1437.htm.

Randa, Sigrid. *Interieurs im Wandel: Möbel- und Innenarchitekturentwürfe aus den Wettbewerben der Zeitschrift "Innen-Dekoration" 1902–1907*. Leinfelden–Echterdingen, Germany: Alexander Koch, 1986.

Raulet, Gérard, and Burghart Schmidt, eds. *Kritische Theorie des Ornaments*. Berlin: Dietrich Reimer, 2004.

Rukschcio, Burkhardt, and Roland Schachel. *Adolf Loos: Leben und Werk*. 2nd ed. Salzburg and Vienna: Residenz, 1987.

Sarmany-Parsons, Ilona. *Die Macht der Kunstkritik: Ludwig Hevesi und die Wiener Moderne*. Göttingen: Vandenhoeck & Ruprecht, 2022.

Scheidl, Inge. "Hugo Gorge." Architektenlexikon, Architekturzentrum Wien. Accessed 31 January 2024. https://www.architektenlexikon.at/de/178.htm.

Sekler, Eduard F. *Josef Hoffmann: The Architectural Work; Monograph and Catalogue of Works*. Princeton, NJ: Princeton University Press, 1985.

Shapira, Elana, ed. *Design Dialogue: Jews, Culture and Viennese Modernism / Design Dialog: Juden, Kultur und Wiener Moderne*. Vienna: Böhlau, 2018.

———. *Style and Seduction: Jewish Patrons, Architecture, and Design in Fin de Siècle Vienna*. Waltham, MA: Brandeis University Press, 2016.

Stoklaska, Juliane. "Oskar Strnad." PhD diss. Universität Wien, 1960.

Spalt, Johannes, and Hermann Czech, eds. *Josef Frank 1885–1967*. Exh. cat. Vienna: Hochschule für angewandte Kunst, 1981.

Spalt, Johannes, and Manfred Wagner, eds. *Der Architekt Oskar Strnad zum hundertsten Geburtstag am 26. Oktober 1979*. Exh. cat. Vienna: Hochschule für angewandte Kunst, 1979.

Thun-Hohenstein, Christoph, Matthias Boeckl, Rainald Franz, and Christian Witt-Dörring, eds. *Josef Hoffmann, 1870–1956: Fortschritt durch Schönheit*. Exh. cat. Vienna: MAK-Museum für angewandte Kunst; Basel: Birkhäuser, 2022.

Wallner, Martina. *Haus & Garten–Frank & Wlach: Ein Beitrag zur österreichischen Wohnkultur*. Graz: Technische Universität Graz, [2009].

Weich, Ulla. "Die theoretischen Ansichten des Architekten und Lehrers Oskar Strnad." Diplomarbeit, Universität Wien, 1995.

Witt-Dörring, Christian. *Josef Hoffmann Interiors, 1902–1913*. Exh. cat. New York: Neue Galerie; Munich: Prestel, 2006.

Zetter-Karner, Katharina, and Christa Zetter, eds. *Wiener Wohnkultur: Josef Hoffmann, Adolf Loos, Kolo Moser, Dagobert Peche, Otto Prutscher, Joseph Urban*. Exh. cat. Vienna: Galerie bei der Albertina, 2015.

Christopher Long | The New Interior

This book was published with assistance from the
Martin S. Kermacy Endowment, School of Architecture,
University of Texas at Austin.

Graphic design
| Jiří Příhoda
Picture editing:
Magdalena Kokešová, Karel Kerlický
Publisher:
| Karel Kerlický – KANT 2024, Prague
www.kant-books.com

KANT

Print:
| PBTisk, Příbram

ISBN: 978-80-7437-429-6